AIR BALL

AIR

JOHN R. GERDY

BALL

**AMERICAN EDUCATION'S
FAILED EXPERIMENT
WITH ELITE ATHLETICS**

UNIVERSITY PRESS OF MISSISSIPPI / JACKSON

www.upress.state.ms.us

The University Press of Mississippi is a member of the
Association of American University Presses.

Copyright © 2006 by University Press of Mississippi
All rights reserved
Manufactured in the United States of America

First edition 2006

∞

Library of Congress Cataloging-in-Publication Data
Gerdy, John R.
   Air ball : American education's failed experiment
with elite athletics / John R. Gerdy.— 1st ed.
      p. cm.
   Includes bibliographical references and index.
   ISBN 1-57806-838-X (cloth : alk. paper)
   1. School sports—United States. 2. College sports—
United States. 3. Sports—United States. I. Title.
GV346.G468   2006
796.04'30973—dc22   2005028429

British Library Cataloging-in-Publication Data available

CONTENTS

ACKNOWLEDGMENTS

Portions of this book are adapted from books and journal articles I have published. For these books and articles, I was the fortunate recipient of valuable comments from colleagues, friends, family, and editors too numerous to mention. There are three, however, who deserve special mention. My thanks go to Cynthia Patterson for her time, perspective, and patience. Her ability to inspire my vision and clarify my thinking is always greatly appreciated. My thanks also go to Steve Mallonee for his prompt and clear answers to my many questions regarding National Collegiate Athletic Association rules and legislative history and to Willie Marble, who always provides much needed amusement.

I am also grateful to my editor, Craig Gill, for his continued belief in and support of my work. Having the opportunity to work with him for a second time has been a pleasure.

Finally, my thanks go to my children, Wallace and James, who make my life joyous and always keep it interesting, and to my wife, Follin, whose love and support make it all possible.

AIR BALL

INTRODUCTION

Every reform was once a private opinion.
—Ralph Waldo Emerson

Each spring, the Southeastern Conference (SEC) convenes its annual meeting in Destin, Florida. The purpose of the gathering is to bring the various members of the SEC "family" together to celebrate the end of the academic year and to review, discuss, and debate conference and National Collegiate Athletic Association (NCAA) policies, issues, and proposals.

The May 1990 meeting promised to be particularly interesting due to a significant national reform agenda that had been laid out by the NCAA's Presidents Commission. Since its inception in 1984, the Commission had aggressively pursued various reform measures, including significant increases in academic standards for athletic eligibility, the establishment of clear presidential authority in athletic matters, and an increased emphasis on more effective oversight of athletics department personnel and programs.

On the legislative agenda at the time was a series of measures designed to improve athlete welfare. This was in response to the release of an NCAA-sponsored survey that revealed that athletes had been underprepared and were underperforming academically, were spending an enormous amount of time on athletics, felt isolated from the general student body, and had little money and time to realize a well-balanced college experience. Among those measures was a proposal to address these feelings of isolation: the elimination of athletic dormitories.

By 1990, there were only a handful of schools housing their athletes in athlete-only dorms. Most of these were in the SEC. Having toured these dormitories during my first year as associate commissioner for compliance and academic affairs, it was easy to understand why athletes felt isolated. While generally upscale as compared to other dormitories, these residence halls were usually located apart from other dorms and close to the athletic complexes. And with athlete-only cafeterias located in the same buildings, the sense of separation and alienation from the general campus community was palpable.

The NCAA proposal to eliminate athletic dorms was designed to promote the integration of athletes into the campus community. National sentiment to eliminate the dorms was overwhelming not only because there were so few remaining, but, more important, the athletic dorm represented what many believed was most wrong about major college athletics. The symbolism of "penning up" mercenary athletes, most of them black, for purposes of monitoring them virtually twenty-four hours a day in an effort to maximize their athletic performance was extremely powerful.

The SEC meetings were structured to allow representatives from each school to meet together with their colleagues. Athletics directors, faculty athletics representatives, senior women's athletics administrators, and presidents met separately to discuss issues for which they were responsible. Also in attendance were the head football coaches as well as the head men's and women's basketball coaches. One item that appeared on each group's agenda was a review and discussion of NCAA legislative proposals. Roy Kramer, newly hired as commissioner, scheduled time to meet with each group to discuss the proposals.

Kramer had previously served as Vanderbilt University's athletics director. He had been very active at the national level, serving on several NCAA committees. Kramer was viewed as someone who could help steer the SEC through what was clearly going to be a tumultuous period. He got a taste of just how tumultuous a period it might be during his meeting with the football coaches.

Given the size of the egos of most SEC football coaches, it was a miracle there was enough room for both Kramer and me to fit inside the conference room. In the Deep South, football coaches are second only to God, and perhaps to the late Dale Earnhardt, as deities to be worshipped. There was no shortage of macho posturing in that room. The largest of a larger than life group was Auburn University's Pat Dye. His program had become dominant in the league and was consistently ranked among the nation's very best. Dye was as old-school, good-ole-boy a football coach as one could get. And he did not like the idea of the NCAA telling him how or where he could house "his players."

To say that Kramer's introduction of the NCAA's proposed ban on athletic dorms prompted a heated debate would be an understatement. The coaches, lead by Dye, were livid. This, they fumed, was something the SEC simply could not allow. No one, not even the NCAA, could tell them what was best for "their players" or "their programs." The last straw was when Kramer tried to explain that, despite what they thought, the measure was going to pass overwhelmingly. In the case of athletic dorms, the SEC was the last of a dying breed. It was inevitable that athletic dorms would be outlawed and Kramer was simply trying to prepare the coaches for that eventuality.

Dye did not want to hear it. Leaning out over the table, he turned to Gene Stallings, the University of Alabama's coach, and drawled, "Gene, do you think we could get the state legislature to pass a law that would require all football players at Auburn and Alabama to live in athletic dorms?"

Stallings cocked his head and replied, "I think we could do that, Pat."

Dye turned back to Kramer and said with a sneer, "What do you think of *that*, Mr. Commissioner?"

Sadly, Dye was probably correct. Alabama and Auburn football was so important to the state and Dye and Stallings were so powerful that they likely could have pulled it off.

The relevance of this story as it applies to athletics reform today lies not in the power of an SEC football coach or the vicelike grip the sport has on the culture of a state, but rather in the degree to which major college athletics can become out of control. It is also an example of tremendous hubris, not only of a football coach but of the athletics enterprise as a whole. That hubris continues today, driven by an attitude best expressed in the words of legendary Alabama coach Paul "Bear" Bryant: "Fifty thousand people don't come to watch an English class." Far too many coaches and athletics administrators continue to believe that athletics is bigger, better, and more important than their educational institution, conference, and even the NCAA.

This story is also an example of how divorced athletics has become from the academic community. Athletic dorms represented the absolute worst in college athletics—athletes treated like cogs in a machine, isolated and separated from the campus community for the sole purpose of keeping them focused on playing ball. That these dorms were used primarily for football and basketball teams, most members of which were black, on overwhelmingly white campuses, further highlighted the "plantation mentality" that permeated many of these programs. On these campuses, it was clear that football and basketball programs had very little to do with education and that the athletics departments had become completely divorced from the academic community. The athletic dorm was the most glaring symbol of that reality.

The fact that Dye may very well have been correct about his power and influence is instructive with regard to the hold that sport has on not only our academic institutions but also our public institutions and cultural values. In many states, particularly in the Deep South, football is not simply a game or a way of life. It is a religion.

Most important, this story provides an example of how all things can, and do, change. Athletic dorms were eliminated. Dye was later forced out as Auburn's coach due to a series of NCAA violations. And, with state and national legislators as well as the public becoming increasingly skeptical regarding the growing commercialization and professionalization of college athletics, it is hard to imagine a state legislature bending to the will of a college football or basketball coach in 2006, even in Alabama.

It is appropriate that a story about college athletics serves as the starting point for a book on how to change the direction and priorities of sport in America. For over three hundred years, Americans have looked to colleges and universities to provide leadership in addressing the critical issues we face as a nation. How we conduct our college athletics programs and the values that are demonstrated through that process filter down to all levels of sport. When our institutions of higher education tacitly endorse activities that glorify athletics at the expense of educational priorities and academic excellence, they provide an example for all to follow. In short, the public looks to higher education to provide educational leadership, including leadership regarding the role, importance, and purpose of sport in our culture.

For this reason, it is higher education that is most responsible for the failure of athletics to meet the educational and public health needs of America. This failure, coupled with higher education's leadership role in our culture, makes it quite clear that if we are ever going to begin the process of establishing a cultural consensus regarding the proper role of sport in our society it is up to the higher education community to initiate it. Perhaps this is an unfair burden. After all, professional sport also bears some responsibility. Maybe so, but not nearly to the degree that higher education does. Higher education's responsibility is greater because, in the case of the cultural area of athletics, higher education has failed in its public mission. We have not provided the necessary leadership in establishing a healthy societal attitude regarding the role that athletics should play in our schools, communities, and lives.

The purpose of this book, however, is not to dwell on the negative impact of a failed system. Rather, it is to address what has been the most significant factor preventing meaningful reform of that system: specifically, the belief that truly significant reform is simply not possible because our addiction to big-time sports has become complete; because the culture of elite sports in America has become so ingrained into societal and educational institutions, it will never change, regardless of the growing evidence of its negative impact.

Yet, despite these challenges, this is a hopeful book. It is hopeful because most, if not all, of the factors that will drive significant cultural and institutional change of athletics in our schools and colleges are already in place. Although not readily apparent to the casual observer, slowly and quietly the foundation upon which meaningful reform will occur has been built. Through the persistent efforts of many within the educational and athletics communities, a critical mass of people, institutions, and ideas has begun to coalesce around the need for fundamental, structural athletics reform.

It is no longer in doubt that reform of the current elite model of athletics within our educational system must start on our college campuses. (By "elite athletics" I mean competitive programs that cater not to the broad population of students who want to pursue athletics as an extracurricular activity, but rather to a select group of highly accomplished athletes, such as those sponsored at the NCAA Division I level, highly competitive high school programs, and youth league "select" teams. When I refer to "elite" athletes, I have in mind the top 1 or 2 percent who aspire to play at the major college level or in the pros.) To that end, college presidents are assuming their rightful responsibility to lead that reform effort. Further, presidents have finally gained control over the NCAA legislative and governance processes necessary to do so. Other groups, such as faculty and trustees, are beginning to recognize their responsibilities in the reform process and have begun to step forward to meet them. And the economic, educational, cultural, legal, and governmental contexts in which these reform efforts are being played out have changed dramatically over the past twenty years. Although many have yet to recognize it, the critical mass necessary to drive fundamental, systemic reform of elite athletics in America's educational system is in place. All that is needed is a spark, whether from an event, an individual, or a group, to ignite the fire of reform.

The purpose of this book is to gather all of the disparate strands of reform and weave them into a coherent vision and logical plan for action. The necessary ingredients to drive and support progressive, systemic change are in place. They simply must be assembled, organized, contextualized, and acted upon. The environment for reform has never been more favorable to the possibility of fundamental change.

It is time to acknowledge that American education's experiment with elite athletics has failed. Its negative impact on our academic values, educational institutions, and cultural priorities can no longer be ignored or rationalized away. We simply can not allow this experiment to continue on its current path. We must boldly deal with the issue. And reform will happen. How and why it will happen will be outlined in the pages to follow.

AN EXPERIMENT JUSTIFIED

I love fools' experiments; I am always
making them.

—Charles Darwin

Elite athletics was incorporated into
our educational system for several
reasons. It was believed that involvement in athletics was
educational for, and built the "character" of, participants.
Further, athletics could also provide entertainment and
serve a unifying function for the school and surrounding
communities, generating positive school and community
spirit. Finally, it was believed that participation in athletics
would not only be healthy for the athletes but would serve
an important public health function by promoting awareness of the value of being fit.

These justifications applied to athletics at both the high
school and college levels. But high schools and colleges each
had additional, unique reasons for embracing elite athletics. Despite idealized notions to the contrary, the most significant reason athletics was incorporated into our high
schools had little to do with education in the traditional
sense. The driving force behind the development of such

programs was the great industrialists of the early 1900s. But rather than having an interest in educating through sport, these business leaders looked upon organized athletics as a means to train, socialize, and control a workforce. Industrial America required workers to be loyal, dependable, physically fit, team oriented, and, above all else, obedient. Sport, it was believed, instilled these characteristics. In the minds of Andrew Carnegie, J. D. Rockefeller, and the like, there was little room for lofty thinking on the assembly line. Factory owners of that time did not want their line workers to be great thinkers, preferring them to passively conform: "The leaders of American industry felt that their workers needed to be loyal and punctual, but not necessarily good academically" (Miracle and Rees, 1994, p. 178).

In the case of higher education, it was believed that athletics could contribute to institutional mission through resource acquisition in the form of money, widespread visibility, increased student enrollment, and enhanced alumni support. Until the late 1800s, university athletics were operated by student-run associations. Students were responsible for arranging travel, securing equipment, and generally administrating the teams. Athletics was simply an institutional afterthought, an activity to keep students amused, but certainly not critical to the educational mission of the university. It was the constant search for resources, coupled with the rapidly growing public interest in athletics and their resultant capability to generate revenue, that convinced presidents and boards to formally incorporate athletics into the structure of their institutions.

Incorporating elite athletics programs into our educational system represents one of the most significant experiments in the history of American education. It can be categorized as an experiment because, at the time, there was no solid empirical evidence to support the reasons used to justify athletics' place in the academy. While the justifications used were certainly plausible and, indeed, desirable, they were guesses, with no research or track record to substantiate them.

Looming over all of these justifications was a basic assumption regarding the role that athletics would play in the institution. It was assumed that the benefits of elite athletics could be achieved in a way that would supplement rather than undermine the academic values and the educational mission of institutions. While some faculty members warned that the marriage of highly competitive, elite athletics with academe was fraught with danger, it was taken largely as a matter of faith that, on balance, athletics would be a positive contributor to an institution's mission. This was an enormous leap because there were no examples in other countries where the responsibility for developing elite athletes and teams rested with the educational system. The marriage of highly competitive, elite athletics and the educational system was a uniquely American experiment.

It has been an experiment that has had an impact far beyond the walls of the academy, greatly influencing our culture and societal values. Virtually every American has been impacted or influenced by high school or college athletics. Whether as a participant, fan, or student, high school and college sports have influenced our attitudes regarding the role that athletics should play in our lives, families, communities, and country.

Now, more than a century later, has the experiment been successful? How effective have our athletics programs been in fulfilling the long-held justifications for their incorporation into our educational system? Sadly, not very effective at all. American education's experiment with elite athletics has been a failure.

THE PRICE HIGHER EDUCATION PAYS

From the involvement of the president of St. Bonaventure University in academic fraud to the murder of a Baylor University basketball player by a teammate and subsequent attempt by the head coach to mislead investigators, there is no shortage of examples of how athletics undermines academic values and educational mission. These transgressions are symptomatic of a larger problem—the alienation of athletics from the university's mission and this trend's impact on public trust in higher education. As the Knight Foundation Commission on Intercollegiate Athletics stated in its 2001 report titled *A Call to Action: Reconnecting College Sports and Higher Education*, "[T]he cultural sea change is now complete. Big-time college football and basketball have been thoroughly professionalized and commercialized" (p. 23).

When the hypocrisy of big-time, NCAA Division I football and basketball being justified on educational grounds is revealed, athletics' negative impact on American higher education is apparent. The effect of this hypocrisy is particularly pernicious because athletics is the clearest window through which the public views higher education. Athletics, particularly big-time NCAA Division I athletics, is extremely popular. Media coverage through newspapers, television, and the internet is extensive. Athletics scandals receive an unprecedented amount of attention and coverage. The result is that college athletics' profile within our national consciousness has risen to an extraordinary level. In short, the consequences for higher education of sponsoring this highly visible hypocrisy are enormous. If the public sees athletics departments with little integrity, how can that same public have faith in higher education's ability to effectively address more pressing societal problems?

The purpose of this book, however, is not to dwell on, sensationalize, or revel in the failure of the current model of elite athletics in America, with its now all-too-extensive and familiar laundry list of examples of academic fraud, uncontrolled spending, institutional lies and cover-ups, recruiting scandals, illiterate athletes, lack of institutional control and integrity, and out-of-control boosters, coaches, and fans. Such examples have become a part of the college athletics landscape and there is simply no need to repeat here what has been written about so extensively elsewhere. That said, however, the current model's shortcomings must be articulated and a few long-held and widely accepted beliefs regarding the value of college athletics must be considered briefly because they relate directly to the fundamental purposes on which the athletics enterprise is founded.

SHATTERING MYTHS

Despite the fact that economics was the primary reason athletics was formally incorporated into American higher education institutions, the NCAA continues to promote

the education of athletes and athletics' effectiveness in supplementing the academic mission of the institution as its
fundamental purposes. Unfortunately, the gulf between the
athletics and academic cultures on our college campuses
has become so wide that we can simply no longer pretend
that athletics is effectively accomplishing these goals.

Institutions recruit athletes who are not prepared for college work and then place athletic demands upon them that
allow little time for academics. Many are placed in "crib"
courses and/or "bogus" majors. Far too many coaches are
more interested in winning games, making money, and
being media personalities than in meeting their responsibilities as educators. Consistently low graduation rates for
athletes, particularly black athletes, in football and men's
basketball offer evidence of this disconnect. Athletics scandals severely damage the reputation of an institution and
erode public trust in higher education. And skewed institutional priorities are on display for all to see when palatial arenas and athletics offices are built while classrooms
and laboratories lack basic amenities and coaches are paid
more than university presidents. As these trends continue,
it becomes more difficult to make the case that elite college
athletics supplements the educational process of the athlete
and the academic mission of the institution.

Another widely held belief regarding athletics departments is that they generate money and resources for the
institution. A first glance would suggest that, from an economic standpoint, college athletics is booming. Basketball and football games can be seen on television virtually every night of the week. CBS paid the NCAA more
than $6.2 billion for the rights to telecast the NCAA men's

basketball tournament for eleven years. Conference championship, football bowl, and basketball tournament games generate millions of dollars for participating institutions and their conferences. Corporations pay millions of dollars for event sponsorship rights and stadium skyboxes. There are now two twenty-four-hour college sports cable networks (ESPN-U and College Sports Television). Colleges also rake in millions from the sale of sports apparel and related merchandise. Corporate logos are plastered on fields, courts, equipment, and uniforms, while coaches are paid hundreds of thousands of dollars to hawk products. Athletics department budgets are bigger, as are stadiums and arenas.

Despite this apparent bonanza, only 18 percent of Division I athletics departments generate more revenue than they expend (Fulks, 2001, pp. 28, 46, 64). Of Division II institutions, less than 6 percent reported a profit (Fulks, 2001, pp. 81, 99). And department costs, as high as they are, may not yet be telling the entire financial story, as many indirect or overhead athletics costs (for example, buildings and grounds maintenance, security, coaches salaries, athletic scholarships) are often paid through the institutional budget. So, the idea that athletics departments are financial engines for universities is misguided. While the profitability of an athletics department may not be a major concern at those schools where athletics is an institutional budget item (largely NCAA Division III institutions), it does raise concerns at institutions that have established programs intended to produce revenue.

It is unfair, however, to evaluate an athletics department's performance on dollars alone. Thus, we have come to accept another major assumption regarding athletics' institutional impact. Athletics, it is said, generates resources in the form of student enrollment, alumni giving, visibility, and public relations. While it is logical that athletics would contribute to the institution in these ways, it is becoming increasingly clear that even in these areas athletics is simply not delivering on its promise.

For example, recent data contradicts one of the strongest myths about college athletics—that winning teams, and especially winning football teams, have a large, positive impact on rates of philanthropic giving at universities that operate big-time programs. Further, when asked which institutional priorities they would like emphasized more and which they would like emphasized less, alumni "voted" for placing *less* emphasis, not more, on intercollegiate athletics. Those who made the biggest donations assigned lower priority to intercollegiate athletics than to nearly every other aspect of college or university life they were asked to rank (Shulman and Bowen, 2001, pp. 220, 201, 226).

The idea that athletics positively impacts a potential student's choice of institution is also a myth. According to a study of college-bound seniors in the spring of 2000 by the Art & Science Group, a research company in Baltimore, most students' awareness of intercollegiate athletics was extremely superficial. Neither the quality nor divisional affiliation of a school's sports program was important to them. Intramural and recreational sports offerings, for example, had a much greater influence on college choice than the intercollegiate athletics program. Students rated jobs, internships, student clubs and organizations, and intramural sports as activities that are more important to them in choosing a college (Suggs, 2001, p. A-51). The fact is most institutions will continue to attract quality students who, when they graduate, will donate money to their alma maters with little regard to the quality or even existence of a big-time athletics program. The claim that athletics programs serve a unifying function for an educational institution also can be disputed.

There are just as many students, faculty, parents, and taxpayers who would rather see institutional resources and energy devoted to improving their school's art, science, theater, or English departments than to renovating a football stadium to include skyboxes that will be utilized less than ten games a year. Furthermore, there are risks in relying on athletics teams to unify educational communities. Schools that use athletics to solve the problems of a fragmented community run the risk of making athletics, not educational and academic excellence, the primary purpose of the institution. Although a football or basketball program can unite a school in a way that an English department cannot, the primary purpose of the institution remains, as it always has been, educational. In short, a winning football team does not make a quality educational institution.

Another justification for the use of athletics is that it generates important resources for the university in the form of visibility and public relations. While there is no denying that athletics can generate significant public exposure and visibility for universities, the larger question is what message is higher education sending to the public through its sponsorship of elite athletics programs? Is it a message that promotes positive academic ideals and principles or rather one that reeks of the hypocrisy of pursuing athletics glory and money at any cost?

The most obvious example of the negative visibility associated with our current elite model of college athletics is the national media coverage that accompanies an athletic scandal. Beyond that, however, there are indications that the public views athletics and the NCAA in ways harmful to higher education. For example, a 2002 NCAA study found that education is not strongly linked with the NCAA image and that most of the public believes that for the NCAA assuring student-athletes get a degree is a low priority. Further, the image of the NCAA is directly linked with connotations of big business and money and the assumption that schools "cheat all the time" (p. 22).

One needs only to watch a televised college football or basketball game to realize that Division I athletics visibility does little to promote educational values or higher education's mission. College sports is packaged, marketed, and projected purely as entertainment with the promotion of educational themes, values, and information an afterthought at best. It is easy to see why televised college sports are overwhelmingly geared to promote athletics. The management of this aspect of athletics programs has always been left to coaches, athletics directors, conference commissioners, and television executives, the very people who are most personally vested in the current model. As a result, televised college athletics has never been considered an opportunity to interface with the public in an educational context. Instead, it is simply one game after another, all devoid of any larger educational purpose or vision— just like the pros.

In short, the use of the elite, professional model of athletics as a commercial vehicle to increase visibility and public relations comes at a high cost to higher education. This cost comes in the repeated failures to promote education and the pervasive negative public opinion regarding the hypocrisy of universities and the NCAA claiming to be about education while operating professional sports franchises.

Another long-held assumption regarding college athletics is that they are a problem only at big-time NCAA Division I institutions. This belief has been particularly harmful because it provides an easy excuse for presidents, faculty, and students at all but the one hundred or so schools at the NCAA Division I-A level to turn a blind eye to athletics' impact on campus values. "Athletics isn't a problem at my school," they say. Meanwhile, the public has come to accept the idea that athletics abuses occur only at a very small percentage of our nation's colleges and universities.

We now know that notion is a myth as well. Two important books, *The Game of Life: College Sports and Educational Values* by James Shulman and William Bowen, along with a follow-up book by Bowen and Sarah Levin entitled *Reclaiming the Game: College Sports and Educational Values*, document the fact that the gap between sport and education is widening not only at Division I institutions but at virtually every institution sponsoring intercollegiate athletics, including Ivy League and select liberal arts colleges. These books, released in 2001 and 2003, respectively, analyze data on ninety thousand students who attended thirty selective colleges and universities over the course of forty years. Combining their research with other historical research and data on alumni giving and budgetary spending on athletics, the authors shatter some very basic assumptions regarding the impact of athletics on institutional culture and academic values.

Specifically, the authors maintain that despite the almost universal acceptance of the notion that issues of college athletic reform apply to big-time football and basketball only, a distinct "athletic culture" is appearing in essentially *all* sports at *all* levels of play, including Division III coed liberal arts colleges. This culture tends to separate athletes from other students and exacerbates the problem of poor academic performance, raising even more difficult questions of educational policy for small private colleges and highly selective universities than for big-time scholarship-granting schools (Shulman and Bowen, 2001, p. 82).

It is particularly noteworthy that these findings apply to schools at all levels of play. In fact, sports' impact on admissions and academic performance may be more significant at small liberal arts colleges and Ivy League institutions because athletes make up a larger percentage of the student population. "The impact of sports programs at places like these may not be as visible on national television, but it can, nevertheless, end up being more consequential" (Shulman and Bowen, 2001, p. 203). This revelation broadens the debate about the potential pitfalls of sponsoring competitive intercollegiate athletics from one concerning major college, full-scholarship programs such as the University of Michigan's to one including nonscholarship, Division III programs such as Williams College's.

Perhaps most disturbing is that in virtually every category, these negative effects are becoming greater. This is so because the intensity of everything connected to the athletics experience, from recruiting, to individual commitment to the sport, to the level of play, has increased at every level, from peewee to professional leagues, all driven by the increasingly professionalized nature of the entire sports system. The result is that the chasm between athletics values and priorities and those of the academic community, always apparent, is becoming greater.

Herein lies the conundrum. At a time when college athletics appears to be more popular than ever, do institutions continue to sponsor their programs as currently structured, despite the fact that their alleged benefits are not being realized and that most of the rationales upon which these programs have been built are not being met?

Again, the purpose of this short review was not to dwell on the scandals and hypocrisies that have become an accepted part of college athletics. It is clear that these highly visible incidents inflict tremendous damage on the integrity of the institution and erode public trust in higher education. But the point must be made: higher education's sponsorship of elite athletics has been a failure. What other conclusion can be drawn when virtually all of its alleged benefits are not being realized and all of the fundamental justifications for its incorporation into academe have, for the most part, been proven to be myths?

BEYOND THE IVY-COVERED WALLS

Disorder in the house, there's a flaw in the
  system
And the fly in the ointment's gonna bring the
  whole thing down
The floodgates are open, we've let the demons
  loose.
The big guns have spoken, and we've fallen for
  the ruse.

—Warren Zevon and George Calderon

The road to reform of America's model of elite athletics begins and ends on the college campus. Between those two points, however, that road runs through our high schools, cuts through our communities, and winds throughout our society.

This is not to say that our high school and community-based sports programs and their administrators, coaches, athletes, and parents have no role to play in reform. All over the country, individuals and institutions at these levels are pushing for and, in many cases, making progress in reforming sports. Unfortunately, locally based initiatives will never add up to drive the type of sweeping, systemic change outlined in the pages to follow. For many reasons, the prospect for broad-based change at these levels hinges on efforts to reform college athletics. As mentioned in the introduction, the examples set and values projected by college programs filter down to the high school, junior high school, and peewee league levels. That same role model capability can also serve as a catalyst for change. Americans look to higher education to provide leadership and direction in addressing the critical issues of the day, including the role that sports plays in our schools, communities, and lives. If we are ever going to improve the way we, as a country, utilize athletics as an educational, public health, and cultural resource, the initiative for that change must come from higher education.

Second, there are powerful cultural forces and structural limitations inherent in high school and community-based athletic systems that prevent such sweeping change. Resistance to change at the high school and community level will be enormous because these institutions of sport are so ingrained in the fabric of the local community. For example, it is tough to imagine high schools in Texas switching to the European club system of community sports without significant influence from an outside force. Further, the administrative and governance structure necessary to drive sweeping national reform of high school and youth league sports simply does not exist. High school athletics is governed and administered at the state level and youth sports at the community level. The prospect of organizing these disparate elements into any coordinated reform effort is highly unlikely. But if the philosophy and operating principles of college athletics were fundamentally reformed, our state high school associations and local youth sports organizations would surely note the example and might feel pressured to initiate their own reforms.

Because college athletics operates under a national umbrella, governed by single national entities (NCAA, National Junior College Athletic Association [NJCAA], and National Association of Intercollegiate Athletics [NAIA]), a coordinated reform effort is quite achievable. As will be documented later, such a movement is currently under way. Over the past twenty-four years, through the persistent efforts of college and university presidents, a critical mass of people and organizations has been coalescing around the idea of athletics reform. This, coupled with a series of changing contextual factors, which will be detailed in chapter four has, for the first time, created an environment where progressive, systemic reform of the college model is within reach.

In short, higher education assumes a significant leadership role in our society and thus bears significant responsibility for the current state of athletics in America. This, coupled with the fact that the system to achieve national reform exists, not at the high school or youth levels, but at the university level, means that the road to reform begins and ends at higher education's doorstep. As a result of the combination of these dynamics, college athletics reform is no longer about academic fraud, illegal payments, over-commercialization, and skyrocketing coaches' contracts. Today, college athletic reform is about the role that sports plays in our lives, schools, and communities. It is about the values we will pass on to our children. It is about public health. It is about reaffirming the importance of education for our personal and national well being. In other words, reform is no longer about what transpires within the ivy-covered walls of academe but rather its societal impact beyond those walls.

The purpose of this chapter is to discuss and understand that broader impact. If we do not understand and appreciate the pervasive impact of college athletics on our high schools and our society, it will be difficult to generate and sustain the sense of urgency and resolve necessary to initiate the type of sweeping change necessary to reform the role of athletics, not only on our college campuses but in American society. First, here is a clarification.

This book is about reforming America's system of sport, from peewee leagues to our college campuses. In chapter one, we examined the negative impact of the elite, professional model on higher education. In this chapter, we will examine its impact on high schools and American society. But to simply criticize the current system without offering prescriptions and alternative models is irresponsible. Because the impetus for cultural change of the magnitude that will be proposed must come from the higher education community, the focus of those reform initiatives will be almost exclusively on college athletics. This is not to diminish the need for reform at the high school or community-sports levels. Rather, it is simply to recognize the reality of the cultural and structural landscape mentioned above. Our colleges and universities must provide the example so that an honest dialogue regarding the role of sports at the high school level and in our communities can begin in earnest. With dialogue comes the potential for increased understanding and future change. But only when we reform college athletics will opportunities begin to present themselves for reforming high school and peewee sports and for rethinking the role that sports plays in our lives and communities.

RETHINKING THE ROLE OF ATHLETICS IN HIGH SCHOOLS

The argument for America's failed experiment with elite high school sports is not nearly as straightforward as it is for college athletics. High school athletics remain largely a local phenomenon compared with the highly visible, nationwide attention that is heaped upon college athletics. Whereas a case of academic fraud at a high school in Minnetonka, Minnesota, may be played out in local and state newspapers and airwaves, an academic scandal at the University of Minnesota would receive exhaustive national coverage.

But the fact that interscholastic sports' impact on high schools is more subtle does not mean it is any less profound. Just as the sponsorship of elite athletics undermines the ability of our colleges and universities to fulfill their mission of providing leadership in addressing the societal issues of the day, the heavy emphasis on interscholastic athletics undermines the ability of our schools to meet the educational and public health needs of our communities.

When thinking of the hypocrisies of college athletics, we tend to focus on the direct impact on the athlete. Specifically, the hypocrisy in the NCAA's use of the term "student-athlete" when it is plain to see that the real reason these young people are on campus is to play ball is very stark. (For this reason, the term "student-athlete" is not used in this book. The NCAA created the term in the 1950s to deflect the threat that its scholarship policy might lead to athletes being regarded as employees and thus be eligible for workmen's compensation insurance. The more honest and accurate term "athlete" or "player" will be employed.) This is particularly true in the high-visibility, high-pressure, revenue-generating sports of football and basketball (although evidence suggests that other sports are heading in the same direction). In these sports, the negative educational impact on the athlete is very visible and direct. Many are not prepared for college work and once on campus, their sports responsibilities leave little time for academics. Amid all the hoopla of the Final Four and football bowl season, it is clear that athletes are paying the biggest price and bearing the heaviest burden for higher education's hypocritical relationship with elite athletics. That cost comes in the form of the false promise of a legitimate educational experience. The impact of this hypocrisy on the general student body and broader university goals, however, is less direct and not as immediately apparent.

At the high school level, this relationship is reversed. With athletes being forced to specialize in a particular sport at earlier ages, high school games being televised nationally, and elite teams touring the country, high school athletics are following the same road to professionalization as college athletics. Regardless, the high school athletic experience remains relatively well balanced. The key to maintaining this relative balance is that the players do not receive athletic scholarships. Therefore, coaches can not act as if they own the athlete. As the college model has shown, when coaches provide athletic scholarships they feel justified in controlling virtually every aspect of "their" athletes' lives. With far less money at stake, high school athletics is not nearly as pressure packed and all-consuming as college athletics. As a result, the educational values and benefits that a well-balanced athletic experience can provide are more likely to manifest themselves at the high school level.

While the high school athlete's experience is more balanced, the negative impact of interscholastic athletics on the general student body and educational mission of the high school is much more profound. High schools have made a huge investment in sports, an investment that is far greater than the public has been lead to believe. Most parents and taxpayers have little understanding of the real costs of athletics. They also have been provided misleading statistics on the number of students actually served by high school sports. But the impact of sports on a school's budget and its athletes tells only part of the story. Elite interscholastic athletics influences in very dramatic ways not only the educational opportunity afforded by a high school but also the health and fitness of every student in the school. Though less visible than at the college level, athletics' impact on the high school is just as profound and far reaching.

SHOW ME THE MONEY!

Determining the cost of interscholastic athletics is extremely difficult. Etta Kralovec, in her 2003 book *Schools That Do Too Much*, offers a cogent critique of why it is hard to develop an accurate picture of the resources consumed by high school athletic programs:

"Calculating the time costs of sports programs in schools, especially at the high school level, is complicated: the culture of sports in many schools means that there is time for pep rallies, away games, homecoming week, and the like and these consume a good part of the school year. Time lost to extracurricular activities is a universal complaint of educators, but researchers have yet to accurately quantify the time spent in sports-related activities. Calculating the money costs of sports programs is even more difficult" (p. 71).

Because athletic expenses rarely appear as a specific line item in a school or district budget, it is nearly impossible to easily obtain an accurate picture of the money and resources spent on sports. Transportation expenses for the football team, for example, are usually included in the transportation costs for the entire district. Insurance costs for athletics are usually meshed with the total insurance bill for the district. Maintenance fees for athletics facilities are generally rolled into the general budget. In most cases, these expenses are considered part of the "extracurricular activities" budget, which adds another layer through which to dig to determine exact athletics costs.

While it is often difficult to determine the percentage of extracurricular spending allocated to sports, it can, with great effort, be done. If the state of New Jersey is any indication of the norm, that percentage is very high.

Based upon data provided by the New Jersey Department of Education, a significant majority of high school extracurricular spending during the 2000–2001 academic year was allocated to interscholastic athletics (Everson, 2002). Extracurricular activities were defined as activities that were not directly related to academic classes, such as band, orchestra, various clubs, yearbook, and field trips. The state does not require each district to report a separate tabulation of budgets for primary, middle, and high schools. However, there were twenty-nine high schools in districts that organized budgets in this way. Of the twenty-nine high schools where spending was calculated for grades 9–12, the percentage of extracurricular spending devoted to athletics ranged from 62 percent to 95 percent. The following is a breakdown of these twenty-nine New Jersey high schools, showing what percentage of their extracurricular budgets they spent on athletics, within various ranges:

PERCENTAGE OF EXTRA-CURRICULAR BUDGET SPENT ON ATHLETICS	NUMBER OF NEW JERSEY HIGH SCHOOLS REPORTING ATHLETICS SPENDING
60–65%	4
66–70%	1
71–75%	3
76–80%	15
81–85%	3
86–90%	1
91–95%	2

For twenty-one out of the twenty-nine schools reporting spending for grades 9–12 (72 percent), almost three-quarters of the schools' extracurricular budgets were spent on interscholastic athletics. These numbers are significant for two reasons. First, we continue to spend the vast majority of our extracurricular resources on elite athletics despite the fact that a much smaller percentage of the student body is involved in such programs than we have been lead to believe. Most figures for high school sports participation, including those published annually by the National Federation of State High School Associations, include the total number of athletes by sport, without taking into account multisport participants.

When Kralovec (2003) asked her local school administrator for the number of athletes at his school, "he proudly talked about the many kids who play sports. School administrators felt that whatever the cost, it was a small price to pay for the number of kids served by sports programs. I was told that out of the 450 kids in the school, well over 300 kids were enrolled in the sports program. But when I looked at the list of participants, the same 80 to 100 students showed up on the team lists. So what looked like 300 students enrolled in sports was actually about 95 students enrolled in three sports each" (p. 73).

There is also increasing evidence of other extracurricular activities and programs that offer a far better return on the educational dollar than elite athletics do. For example, a strong case can be made that music programs yield a far greater return on educational dollars invested in them than do elite sports teams. While it takes more physical strength, conditioning, and agility to dunk a basketball, the traits necessary to be a successful athlete—discipline, hard work, perseverance, teamwork—are identical to those required to be a successful musician. In short, both music and athletics can contribute significantly to the character development of participants. Music, however, offers something that highly competitive, organized sports do not; a direct link between participation and intellectual development, as a growing body of evidence indicates that arts instruction can significantly strengthen students' academic performance.

While it is difficult to determine the amount of resources devoted to sports, what is certain is that the actual cost, in terms of money alone, is far greater than has been portrayed. Kralovec (2003) described her experience of working with a local school board member in analyzing the budget:

> By his calculations when you include transportation, maintenance, insurance, and operations costs, the total cost of competitive athletics in my district is closer to 10 percent (versus the 5 percent identified, listed costs in the budget) of the total school budget, or $500,000.
>
> So we see that the full costs of the competitive athletic program are not publicly disclosed, can be fully analyzed only with great effort and, as a result, are rarely questioned. Even the Finance Center of the Consortium for Policy Research in Education (CPRE), which has conducted the most comprehensive analysis of the education dollar, did not break out the costs of athletic programs in high schools. (pp. 73)

While the impact of sports on the educational institution can be debated, there is no arguing with the fact that with far fewer students being served by sports than has been portrayed the cost of interscholastic athletics is far greater than previously imagined. With our schools facing an increasingly difficult funding and economic climate, the implications of this more realistic assessment of athletics department costs are significant.

READING, WRITING, AND ARITHMETIC

The fundamental purpose of secondary education in America is teaching and learning. Thus, it is no surprise that the primary justification for the sponsorship of high school athletics was the notion that participation was a way in which to supplement the educational process. To justify the time, emotion, and resources spent on athletics, it had to be clear that they contributed not only to the educational development of the individual athlete but also to the general teaching mission of the institution. Sadly, high school athletics are evolving in a way in which their positive educational impact on the athlete is diminishing while their negative impact on the general student body and teaching mission of the school is increasing. Specifically, there are significant costs resulting from the impact of the culture of sport on a high school's academic values and priorities.

The extent to which organized sports subverts our nation's educational interests is enormous. At the grade school and high school levels, this subversion involves the passing of athletes who have not mastered the work. The prevailing notion is that it is acceptable if Johnny can't read as long as he can play. Coaches plead the case of a "good kid, whose only chance at a better life is through an athletic scholarship and he won't be eligible unless he passes this course." Far too often, the teacher or principal complies, not wanting to be responsible for denying a youngster his "only chance." Unfortunately, everyone knows—classmates, parents, coaches, teachers and Johnny himself—that Johnny did not deserve to pass. This significantly impacts the academic credibility of the institution. Such acts, and they are far from isolated, serve to cheapen the value and standing of education in our communities.

H. G. Bissinger, in his 1990 book *Friday Night Lights*, explains how athletics undermined educational priorities at Permian High School in Odessa, Texas. He noted that the cost of boys' medical supplies at Permian was $6,750. The cost for teaching materials for the English department was $5,040, which included supplies, maintenance of the copying machine, and any extra books besides the required texts that a teacher thought might be important for students to read. The cost of game film was $6,400. Meanwhile, the English department had just received its first computer, which was to be used by all twenty-five teachers. An English teacher with twenty years experience earned a salary of $32,000, while the football coach, who also served as athletics director, earned $48,000 and the free use of a new Taurus sedan each year. And, during the 1988 season, Permian spent $70,000 for chartered jets for the football team's travel (pp. 146–47).

Such imbalance prompted one teacher to fume, " 'This community doesn't want academic excellence. It wants a gladiatorial spectacle on Friday nights.' As she made that comment, a history class meeting a few yards down the hall did not have a teacher. The instructor was an assistant football coach. He was one of the best teachers in the school, dedicated and lively, but because of the pressures of preparing for a crucial game, he did not have time to go to class. That wasn't to say however, that the class did not receive a lesson. They learned about American history that day by watching *Butch Cassidy and the Sundance Kid*" (Bissinger, 1990, pp. 147–48). And while in this case the football coach was a good teacher, there are countless examples of teachers being hired not based upon their ability as teachers but upon their skill as coaches. This is simply one example of a culture in many schools that demands nothing less than the best on the fields of play at the expense of excellence in the classroom.

Another way the culture of sports impacts the teaching function of a high school relates to how school days are structured. Typically, the school day starts at 7:30 A.M., is fragmented into many periods with many interruptions throughout, and ends as early as 1:30 P.M. This allows long afternoons for sports practices. There are several problems with this structure. Research suggests that adolescents do not truly wake up until 9:00 A.M. Further, fifty minute class sessions are too short for effective teaching and learning. Finally, the school day ends too early. Ironically, the "subject" that occurs in the best learning environment (a long, uninterrupted period of time in the afternoon) is sports.

According to Kralovec (2003), when you ask a board member about the structure of the school day, "you are likely to hear all kinds of reasons why the teachers' and other unions have set the time schedules the way they have. What school administrators are less willing to admit is that the schedule meets the needs of the competitive athletic program and always has." Further, "since most students do not participate in competitive athletic programs after school, many communities must struggle to find meaningful activities for students for this chunk of time. What is the message we are sending when we reserve the best part of the day for sports?" (p. 24).

"What is perhaps most remarkable about Alexandra's [a fictitious student] day," Kralovec (2003) notes, "is that for a full three hours and fifteen minutes she had a perfect learning environment. No interruptions, a student teacher ratio of one to six, and pedagogical practices that build on an adolescent's developmental need to belong. Was this her math class? Her English class? Her science class? Was this time turned over to intense individual work? Did she work on her intellectual passion for writing a play? Nope, she played sports" (p. 28).

Given that athletes generally represent a small percentage of the student population, assigning the optimum learning environment to sports practice negatively impacts the educational opportunity for the majority of the student body, thus undermining the teaching mission of the school. The structure of the school day, tailored in large part to meet the needs of the athletics department, is an example of distorted educational and community priorities. While high school athletics' impact on the general student body is less visible than the highly publicized, hypocritical relationship between college athletics and the education of the athlete, that impact is just as profound.

THE CHANGING FACE OF HIGH SCHOOL SPORTS

There is a commonly accepted belief of the existence of a causal relationship between high school athletics and educational achievement. While this may be true to a degree, there are some significant developments in the evolution of high school sports suggesting the educational impact on the individual athlete is changing, and not necessarily for the better. For example, the link between the high school coach and the academic community is becoming weaker as the number of coaches who actually teach high school is dwindling.

One of the most enduring impressions of my early 1970s high school athletics and educational experiences was how inextricably linked they were. My educational experience in the classroom and on the basketball court was seamless. This was because all of my coaches were also teachers in the school. I not only interacted with my basketball coach at practice, but also in the classroom. He was my history teacher. The three other members of his coaching staff were also teachers.

My father was a physics teacher as well as the head football coach. While others my age were swimming or riding bikes, I was on the practice field as my father put his teams through preseason drills, in the locker room before and after practice, and on the sidelines during games. I spent a large part of my youth surrounded by coaches, all of whom were also classroom teachers. While they were certainly generous with their time and advice about athletics, what had a more lasting impression on me was the emphasis they placed on education. While they all loved athletics, what drove them was the opportunity to work with young people in a teaching environment. They were teachers who also coached.

After games, the entire coaching staff gathered at our house. I would watch and listen for hours as these coaches rehashed the game, diagramed plays, argued about players and play calls, told stories, laughed, ate, and drank.

While the focus on game day was the game, their conversation often revolved around the school and the education of young people. They were passionate about the young people on their team, not simply as athletes, but as students and as people. They were teachers who were invested in and committed to education and to the school of which they were a part. Most had their master's degrees, having personally invested in the educational process, and years of experience in the classroom. These were people who considered themselves teachers who happened to coach. Teaching was their profession, their passion, and their life's calling.

Today, the link between the athletic fields and the educational institution is much more tenuous. The reason for this breakdown relates directly to the core justification for sports in our high schools. Specifically, it is far more difficult to justify high school athletics being supplemental to the academic process and educational institution and coaches being teachers and educators when a rising number of them do not teach in the schools at which they coach. For many, the only school facilities they enter are the locker room and the playing field or court. This is problematic because there is little opportunity to integrate the coach into the academic community. As a result, many coaches have little appreciation for, or understanding of, educational and academic expectations, practices, philosophies, and mores and no connection to the educational institution and its cultural values.

For whatever reasons (low pay, less willingness to deal with overzealous parents, and others) the number of high school coaches who are professional teachers is declining. Today, a high school coach is just as likely to be a lawyer, salesperson, or mechanic as to be a teacher. According to a 2005 survey conducted by *Reading Eagle* newspaper reporter Mike McGovern, 53 percent (132 of 250) of the middle school and junior high head coaches from the nineteen school districts in Berks County, Pennsylvania, were teachers (2005). Tim Flannery of the National Federation of State High School Associations estimates that 50 percent of high school coaches are not high school teachers. "This number represents a dramatic decline in the number of coaches who are also teachers. It is a matter of great concern," Flannery went on to say (2002).

Many of these coaches have never taught in the classroom and have little training or certification in coaching techniques or philosophy. Their only training is their observations of how others perform the role or their memories from their own high school careers. Often, these coaches model their behavior after professional and college coaches they have seen on television. For obvious reasons this may not be the most appropriate behavior for high school coaches. The result is a weakening link between what occurs on the fields of play and the educational institution because the leader of the sports team—the coach—has no connection to the academic institution. Consequently, the goals, purposes, and culture of the athletic team often run counter to those of the school, specifically, and education generally.

This is not to trivialize the time, effort, and commitment devoted by such individuals to coaching young people. Their efforts should be respected, appreciated, and rewarded. They are certainly not doing it for the money. And there are excellent coaches who are not full-time teachers. There are also full-time teachers who are horrible coaches. That said, there is no ignoring that, on balance, the link between the athletic and educational experience suffers when there is no link between teacher and coach.

Coaches and athletics administrators justify their involvement with young people on the basis that they are educators. The playing field or court, they say, is their classroom, and the lessons taught there in discipline, teamwork, and sportsmanship are just as important as the lessons being taught in the lecture hall, chemistry lab, or at home. This trend in coaching background suggests, however, that a coach's educational commitment and connection to the academic community is becoming less important. In short, it is a sad commentary on the supposed link between athletics and the educational mission of an institution when all one needs to be considered a coach is a whistle.

IT'S SHOW BIZ!

Another indication of the widening gulf between high schools' athletics and academic cultures is increasing evidence that high school sports is becoming less about education and more about entertainment. *USA Today* publishes a national top twenty-five list. The number of high school athletic events that are being televised is rising. Several of LeBron James's high school games were nationally televised on a pay-per-view basis. More schools are traveling out of state to play games or tournaments against other top teams. It is no longer good enough to determine the best team in a league, county, or state; we now have to determine the best team in the country. All of this hype is being urged on by overzealous coaches and parents and by media that care only about feeding our society's sports-crazed obsession and selling newspapers and television-commercial spots. The sports-entertainment culture is filtering further down the athletics food chain and the negative impact of that downward drift on high schools is growing.

Of all the justifications for educational institutions sponsoring athletics, it is the entertainment function that programs are meeting most effectively. Sports are fun to watch. And there is value in sports' entertainment function. This, however, begs the larger question of whether educational institutions should be in the entertainment business, particularly when so many of the values and attitudes of the entertainment culture run counter to those of the educational community. As has occurred at the college level, the entertainment culture of sport has increased pressure on coaches, teachers, and administrators to compromise academic values and educational priorities, which undermines a school's educational mission.

The implications of the entertainment culture's downward creep and the win-at-all-costs philosophy that accompanies it should not be taken lightly because they impact what has long been considered a vital role of sports in schools. Athletics programs can unify educational institutions and communities in ways that the English department can not. This belief drives much of the push toward increased commercialism, visibility, and national-level competition. But just as with college athletics, there are costs and risks in relying on athletic teams to unify a school or community.

AN ISSUE OF HEALTH

While there is much evidence suggesting that elite athletics undermines academic values and the educational

experience of the general student body and compromises a
high school's teaching function, it is in the area of public
health that the current athletics structure fails most dramatically. Lifelong health and fitness habits are not developed
by accident. They must be taught, nurtured, and practiced
regularly from an early age. Our schools must play a role
in this educational process by aggressively teaching and
promoting the concept of fitness for life. The responsibility of schools to begin teaching fitness-for-life concepts
more aggressively is becoming increasingly important as
America has become the most obese nation in the world.
And the health costs resulting from this dubious honor are
staggering.

There are three programmatic formats through which
our schools can affect the health of virtually every child in
America: physical education classes, intramural sports, and
interscholastic athletics. At issue is whether the current relative emphasis placed upon these activities best serves our
nation's health and physical fitness needs. In other words,
what is the most effective and cost-efficient way our school
systems can teach and promote good health and physical
fitness habits to our nation's youth? And are our nation's
health interests being met by the increasing emphasis in
terms of time, effort, emotion, and money that is being
spent on interscholastic athletics as opposed to physical
education requirements and intramural athletics?

The vast majority of health, physical education, and
athletics-related extracurricular school spending funds
interscholastic sports. A large percentage of that total funds
football, a sport in which the final high school contest will
be the last time that 99 percent of the participants ever

play the game. Yet, football flourishes while high school gym class requirements are reduced. The *New York Times* reported in 2000 that in the nation "only 29 percent of high school students had daily physical education in 1999, down from 42 percent in 1991. Two years ago, Virginia stopped requiring physical education in elementary school. In 1966, Massachusetts did so for high school. By 1999, only 61 percent of Massachusetts high school students had gym class even one time per week, down from 80 percent five years earlier" (Rothstein).

Today, Illinois is the only state that still requires daily physical education classes for students in kindergarten through twelfth grade. And Colorado, along with South Dakota, does not have any mandate for physical education on any level—elementary school, middle school, or high school (Reed, 2004). In short, an official policy of encouraging students to pursue a healthy life through exercise is no longer a priority in our nation's schools. Meanwhile, our nation becomes more obese. The Centers for Disease Control and Prevention reports that the percentage of obese children ages six to eleven has increased nearly 300 percent over the last twenty-five years. And the numbers are nearly identical for teenagers (Reed, 2004).

If we believe sport to be a character-building activity that prepares youth for adulthood and instills in them important values and discipline, why is our system of organized athletics not structured to encourage maximum participation? Rather than maximizing opportunities for students to become involved in and reap the positive personal and health benefits of organized athletics, our current system weeds out, at earlier and earlier ages, all but the most talented athletes and, in the process, discourages participation by all but those who display extraordinary potential.

This athletic elitism begins in youth sports leagues with the selection of all-star traveling teams of ten-year-olds and continues through high school and college. The result is that the best perform while all others watch. In this system, there is no encouragement for involvement in sports simply to stay physically fit or to have fun. It is all about preparing the team or the team's star to get to the next level. Children pick up on the exclusive nature of these programs and often stop playing when they realize they are not one of the elite. There is nothing in this model that encourages children to become physically fit themselves or to learn about and enjoy the process of fitness. From peewee leagues to our nation's campuses, encouraging a healthy lifestyle through sport is simply not a priority.

If the desired outcome of scholastic athletics is for participants to have fun, develop character, gain confidence, and improve their health, they must be organized and conducted with these purposes in mind. To maximize sports' potential to positively influence the health and fitness of our children, the focus of our schools' investment in sport should be on involving the greatest number of participants rather than spending an increasing amount of time, money, effort, and emotion on only those who might have the potential to play college or professional sports.

Communities must engage in honest dialogue regarding the role that sports should play in our lives, our schools, and our communities. It is a conversation we can no longer afford to avoid. This dialogue must start with us owning up to the painful fact that, with our schools leading the way, our sport system is badly out of step with our nation's health needs. By investing so heavily in interscholastic sports, our schools have failed to promote the idea that sport for pure exercise is positive, fun, and healthy. We have embraced the notion that athletics must be about winning and developing future all-stars and pros. The cost of this failed policy on the health and fitness of all Americans has been enormous and, like our waistlines, is growing.

IT'S ABOUT TEACHING AND EDUCATION

This leads to another important aspect of the discussion regarding the role of athletics in our secondary schools. Specifically, what is the relationship between athletics participation and the development of the skills necessary to succeed in tomorrow's workplace? Business leaders are expressing increasing concern about the inability of our educational system to develop in workers the skills necessary to keep American companies competitive in the high-tech, information-based, global economy of the future. As our economy becomes less physical and more cerebral, a common complaint is that too much emphasis, not only in terms of dollars but, more importantly, in terms of time and effort, is being placed upon maintaining highly competitive athletics programs, often at the expense of other extracurricular activities and educational programs in music, math, art, foreign languages, or the sciences.

While punctuality, hard work, discipline, a strong body, and the ability to produce in a team environment are all desirable worker traits, preparing our country's workforce to compete successfully in the information-based, service economy of the new millennium will require instilling in students the ability to reason, think creatively, adapt to change, manage large amounts of information, critically assess data, and compute, speak, and write effectively. The "Information Age" will require strong minds developed in classrooms more than strong bodies developed on playing fields. The worker skills Andrew Carnegie considered necessary for advancing America's economic interests in 1906 may not be considered adequate by Bill Gates for advancing America's economic interests in the year 2006 and beyond.

Not only are the skills necessary for economic success changing, but the pool of workers American children must compete against for the jobs of the future is increasing dramatically. Pulitzer Prize–winning author Thomas L. Friedman, in his provocative book *The World Is Flat: A Brief History of the Twenty-First Century* and in other pieces, describes the increased competition as the "flattening" of the world:

> For so many years, America's economy was so dominant on the world stage, so out front in so many key areas, that we fell into the habit of competing largely against ourselves. . . . In recent years, though, with the flattening of the global playing field, it should be apparent that we are not just competing against ourselves. The opening of China, India and Russia means that young people in these countries can increasingly plug and play—connect, collaborate and compete—more easily and cheaply than ever before. And they are.
>
> On April 7, CNET News.com reported the following: "The University of Illinois tied for 17th place in the world finals of the Association for Computing Machinery International Collegiate Programming Contest. That's the lowest ranking for the top-performing U.S. school in the

29 year history of the competition. . . . Earlier this week, a special report on the Indiana University High School survey of Student Engagement, which covered 90,000 high school students in 26 states was published. The study noted that 18 percent of college track seniors did not take a math course in their last year in high school–and that more than a fifth (22 percent) of first year college students require remediation in math. Just 56 percent of the students surveyed said they put a great deal of effort into schoolwork; only 43 percent said they had worked harder than expected."

Martha McCarty, the Indiana University professor who headed the study told me, "Our fear," she added, is that when you talk to employers out there, they say they are not getting the skills they need, in part because "the colleges are not getting students with the skills they need." (Friedman, 2005, p. A-23)

The purpose of this review was to identify and explain the ways elite interscholastic sports impacts the teaching and public health functions of our high schools. As is becoming increasingly apparent, those impacts may not be nearly as positive as has long been assumed. The fact is, as much as we love sports, we must value the education, health, and fitness of our children more. If it is determined that any element of our educational system undermines these education and public health priorities, we must seriously consider how to restructure or eliminate it in favor of programs that promote the desired results and produce a better educational and public health return on dollars invested.

Thus, the question is whether the purpose of high school sports should be to develop elite athletes and teams or to encourage an appreciation for, and development of, good lifelong health, fitness, and personal wellness habits and behaviors through broad-based participation in our citizenship. Should our sports programs be designed to develop our future professional and Olympic athletes or to emphasize learning through participation? In other words, what role should our educational system assume as it relates to the cultural area of athletics?

THE ALL-AMERICAN ADDICTION

No discussion of American education's failed experiment with elite athletics can be considered thorough without acknowledging its impact on our society generally. Our nation's educational institutions occupy a unique place in our culture. While they are a reflection of our societal values and beliefs, they are also looked to for cultural leadership and direction. This dichotomy is reflected in the debate over the role and purpose of athletics in our schools and society.

Sports advocates often claim that high school and college athletics' ills are simply a reflection of broader societal values. While that may be true to some extent, the relationship between sports and society is far more complex. The fact that high school and college athletics have become so visible and influential has had a significant impact on wider cultural values and beliefs. Our educational institutions and cultural values have a symbiotic relationship in which the priorities exhibited by high school and college athletics have a tremendous impact on larger, cultural attitudes and values relating to sports and the role they play in our lives and communities. Unfortunately, that impact on our society has become far too negative. We have lost perspective regarding the role that sports should play in our lives. I characterize that impact in the title of my 2002 book, *Sports: The All-American Addiction*.

Sadly, we have become addicted to sport; it is our society's opiate. We plan our days, weekends, and even vacations around it. If it is on the television anywhere near us, at home, the local bar, or a restaurant, we invariably turn to watch. We cannot even get away from it in our cars as we tune to the incessant wail of sports talk radio. We will do whatever we need to do to get it—twenty-four hours a day, seven days a week, from Key West to Seattle, Maine to Monterey. While a little escapism is not harmful, addiction is. Although not as destructive as an addiction to drugs, educationally, intellectually, or personally, a sports addiction can be very harmful as it lures us into physical inactivity and a mindless stupor.

Like a drug addiction, being a sports fan offers little long-term substance or meaning. It allows us to escape our problems, ignoring the issues that face us, and undermines our attempts to solve them. We invest effort and emotion in sports stars and teams rather than improving our lives by reading, writing, learning a new skill or mastering a musical instrument, or simply engaging in meaningful conversation with a friend or family member. It is not enough to simply watch one game. We must watch the next, and the next. We need to repeat the act again, and again, and again, just to feel normal. And, as with drugs, a sports addiction can adversely affect those around us—friends, spouses, and children. For example, how many thousands of times do conversations come to a standstill the moment a game is turned on? Rather than interacting with a friend or family member, instead our eyes and attention turn to the tube, and we slowly slip into a collective ESPN-induced stupor.

Rather than getting involved, sport makes it easy for us to choose to sit idly and watch, television remote in hand. Sport is what we talk about when we want to avoid thinking or talking about anything meaningful or important. Like crack addicts sitting around their pipe in a dream state waiting for their next "hit," we sit in front of our televisions, unresponsive to the world around us, eyes glazed over, minds numbed, totally absorbed in a sports fantasy "trip," waiting for the next big play.

Yet, we do not mind our addiction. In fact, we embrace it. Sport is pure; it is wholesome; it embodies the "American Way," showcasing champions and providing us with winners to worship and emulate. We do not mind our addiction to sport because it is the All-American Addiction. And because it is All-American, we do not believe we suffer any consequences from it. But we do.

Day after day the sports pages present us with examples of the negative effects of the win-at-any-cost mentality that drives our sports culture. Recruiting scandals undermine academic institutions and intellectual values. In locker rooms and on sidelines, signing a pro contract and buying a fancy sports car is valued far more than earning a college degree. Coaches scream at seven-year-olds for committing an error in a T-ball game. Parents attack Little League umpires or fatally beat each other at youth hockey games. We can no longer play sports simply for fun and exercise; we must elevate all competition to epic proportions. Today's "Game of the Century" is merely a prelude to next week's "Even Bigger Game of the Century." Cheating is rampant.

This is what organized sport has become. This is our All-America Addiction.

DUMB JOCKS IN THE INFORMATION AGE

As with any addiction, elite athletics' negative effects on our culture are far ranging. For example, beyond the negative impact on our schools' and colleges' ability to effectively meet their teaching functions, elite athletics influences the values we instill in our children. Consider, for example, the way we use role models to teach our children certain characteristics and values.

Despite the customary scholar-athlete-of-the-week award, the pervasive image of an athlete is that of being dumb. Why else, for example, did we marvel at, and so many media representatives go to such lengths to explain, the success of Princeton's men's basketball team? How could a group of intelligent Ivy Leaguers be a great basketball team? (McCabe, 2000, p. 142). The message is clear: physicality and intellectualism are conflicting ideals. Yet, we insist on using athletes as role models to be emulated by our children. Is the fact that athletes can run fast and jump high valid reason to encourage our children to model their behavior after them when those skills will be of little value in the information-based twenty-first century global economy? Athletes are not in a position to be role models, particularly *educational* role models. These are, after all, the same people we consider dumb jocks!

And while it takes discipline and hard work to succeed in athletics, the benefits of that success may ultimately distort an individual's work ethic and concept of personal responsibility. From the moment a young person is identified as an outstanding athlete, he or she is coddled, pampered, and in many ways given a free pass through life by coaches, fans, teachers, fellow students, and even his or her parents. As a result, athletes often develop a warped sense of entitlement, expecting everything will either be given to them or taken care of for them, which hardly instills a positive work ethic and a strong sense of personal responsibility.

These are simply a few examples of the ways our infatuation with elite athletics in our schools, colleges, and culture contributes to a society that seems to have lost its sense of the proper relationship between sport and education; between the development of the mind and of the body.

GIVE ME YOUR MONEY!

Our All-American Addiction also economically impacts our communities. For example, most economists who seriously study the economic impact of sports stadiums and franchises agree they are not a good civic investment. Andrew Zimbalist of Smith College and Roger G. Noll of Stanford University edited a book on stadium financing for the Brookings Institution titled *Sports, Jobs, and Taxes*. In it, Zimbalist, Noll, and fifteen collaborators study the issues "from all angles" and contend that, " [a] new sports facility has an extremely small (and perhaps negative) overall effect on overall economic activity and employment. No recent facility appears to have earned anything approaching a reasonable return on investment" (qtd. in Gross, 1999, p. C-6). Zimbalist and Noll say that "even the most successful publicly funded new stadium, Oriole Park at Camden Yards in Baltimore, has resulted in a net gain to the Baltimore economy of only about $3 million a year, not much return on a $200 million investment" (qtd. in Gross, 1999, p. C-6). Yet, despite the increasingly high price we pay to satiate our addiction, we continue to shell out our hard-earned cash. Worse, we continue to justify our investment largely on idealized notions about sports' positive civic impact.

Not only is the economic impact of elite athletics on high schools and colleges far less positive than we have been led to believe, the same holds true for sports' supposed economic impact on our cities and communities. With our communities and educational institutions facing significant challenges in the form of poverty, crime, illiteracy, educational reform, environmental degradation, and the task of preparing our workforce to compete in global, information-based, world markets of the twenty-first century, the question is whether the price tag on our sports obsession has gotten too steep?

THE ATHLETE AS COUCH POTATO
The public health impact of our All-American Addiction reaches far beyond the campus walls. Consider the societal impact of what has now become a national phenomenon, the NCAA men's and women's basketball tournaments. Each March, America is overcome by "madness." Throughout the country, sports fans, both casual and hard-core, focus their attention on the NCAA's men's basketball tournament. In bars and bakeries, at dinner tables and over phone lines, people catch the madness. Office pools are organized

and parties are thrown as television screens everywhere are tuned to "The Big Dance," as teams from Boise to Birmingham, Athens, Georgia, to Athens, Ohio, and New York to New Mexico compete for the national championship.

Dubbed "March Madness" for the unpredictable nature of the contests as well as its catchy commercial ring, this competition has captivated our nation's televised sports consciousness as no other event has. But the term "March Madness" is appropriate for another reason; everyone is *watching* it. If everyone is watching, no one is participating. Instead, fans are sitting in front of the television set stuffing themselves with junk food and beer.

March Madness is the best example of the evolution in the way we "participate" in sports. This shift is problematic because our heavy cultural investment in sport is justified largely upon the claim that it promotes a healthy lifestyle. Unfortunately, the behavior the vast majority of Americans associate with March Madness—watching rather than playing—has a *negative* effect on physical health.

Before televised sports, if parents wanted to share an athletic experience with their child, they would go to the backyard and play catch. Today, it is just as likely that such an experience consists of watching one of the hundreds of televised sporting events each week. Organized sport in America has become more about watching elite athletes perform than about being active oneself, as likely to be associated with lying on a couch as working up a sweat. Television has lured us from the playing fields to the stands. Rather than being in the middle of the action, we observe from afar. Meanwhile, our nation becomes more obese.

The distortion of the value and purpose of sport in our culture has lead to the evolution of a sports system that is badly out of step with our nation's health needs. Rather than maximizing opportunities to become involved in and reap the personal and health benefits of organized athletics, our current system weeds out, at an earlier and earlier age, everyone but those who display extraordinary potential.

In promoting this elitist structure, we have failed to advance the idea that sport for pure exercise is positive, fun, and healthy. Rather, athletics must be about winning and developing future all-stars and pros. If we believe sport to be a character-building activity, an activity that prepares youth for adulthood and instills in them important values and discipline, why is our system of organized athletics not structured to encourage maximum participation?

Even the case for the positive health benefits of participation in competitive athletics may not be as clear cut as it seems. While participation in elite, organized sport requires exercise, it is anything but moderate. In far too many cases, the physical demands and expectations required by competitive athletics borders on abuse. For example, incidences of overuse injuries in young athletes are increasing due to pressure to specialize in a particular sport and commit to year-round training at young ages. "It's not enough that they play on a school team, two travel teams, and go to four camps for their sport in the summer," says Dr. Eric Small, who has a family sports medicine practice in Westchester County, New York. "They have private instructors for that one sport that they see twice a week. Then their parents get them out to practice in the backyard at night" (qtd. in Pennington, 2005, p. 1). "The volume of training has increased beyond the maturing young body's ability to handle it," echoes Dr. Angela Smith, an orthopedic surgeon at the Children's Hospital of Philadelphia (qtd. in Pennington, 2005, p. 1). Because the rewards for winning—wealth, notoriety, adulation, and fame—have become so great, athletes and even their parents are more than willing to place the athlete's lifelong physical health at risk for these immediate but fleeting rewards. Coaches, chasing the same rewards, do nothing to dissuade the athlete from doing so.

For sport to fully maximize its potential to positively affect the health and fitness of our populace, its focus should be upon involving the maximum number of participants rather than spending an increasingly large commitment of money, time, effort, and emotion on only those athletes who might have the potential to play major college or professional sports. In short, we must begin playing more and watching less.

SPORT AND A CIVIL SOCIETY

Finally, there is the impact of our All-American Addiction on the elements necessary for a civil society. For a society to thrive, there must exist among its citizenry a basic set of behavioral norms, ethical standards, and humanistic values. Most discussions of civil society center upon what binds a community: trust, honesty, compassion, and civic responsibility.

It is the promise of a fair contest that forms the foundation upon which all athletic competition is based. Without the element of trust—that a standard set of rules will govern participation—our "games" would cease to exist and be replaced by chaos. This ethical dimension, referred to as "sportsmanship," is sports' most powerful link to America's democratic ideals; it is directly related to the fundamental elements of a civil society.

The erosion in the belief that athletic participation teaches sportsmanship is so extensive that most have come to consider the term "sports ethics" an oxymoron. For example, a 2000 study by the University of Rhode Island's Institute for International Sport found that 26 percent of NCAA Division I basketball players agreed to some extent that their teammates would expect them to cheat if it meant the difference in winning a game. In short, sportsmanship has gone the way of the peach basket and leather football helmet.

While athletes are trained to compete fiercely, they are allegedly also taught to respect their teammates and opponents. These lessons in compassion, empathy, and respect are important principles of a civil society because they influence the way we treat and relate to each other as human beings. It is difficult, however, to find behavior that demonstrates respect for opponents when watching athletics today. The dancing and gyrating that follows even a routine basket or touchdown, the standing over a fallen opponent, and the general in-your-face mentality of many of today's athletes hardly reflects or promotes humility, compassion, and respect for others.

Amidst all the high salaries, self-promotion, and profit-driven priorities and behavior, could it be that the concepts of teamwork and loyalty have become distorted? Professional players jump from one team to another so often that the stadium vendors' cry, "You can't tell the players without a scorecard," has never rung more true. College coaches' concepts of loyalty are shaped more by the size of their financial "package," complete with sneaker deals, television shows, summer camp arrangements, and loaner cars, than by notions of commitment to a university or to education. Organized sport is a free-for-all, governed by a bottom line of "getting mine and getting it now." This sits in stark contrast to the notion that in a civil society an individual has an obligation to the larger community.

A civil society also requires that we have the ability to resolve disputes peacefully. Athletics allegedly contributes to our ability to do so in that it provides a positive outlet for aggression. Today's culture of elite sport however, does far more to glorify violence and aggressive behavior than it does to promote civility and conflict resolution. Athletes are rewarded by coaches for their aggressiveness and combativeness and highlight shows repeatedly air recaps of the most violent, "big hits," all in excruciatingly slow motion. Then, we are shocked when an athlete's aggression spills over from the field to the home.

The values and behavioral standards that exist within the athletics community run counter to those essential to the functioning of a civil society. The in-your-face mentality in what seems to be an increasing number of athletes hardly suggests that sport is teaching humility, empathy, conflict resolution, and compassion for others. Cheating is expected, violence is glorified, and a lack of civility toward competitors is considered a positive attribute. In elite sports, there are no rules of civility. There is no trust. There are no standards of acceptable behavior, or, if there are, they can easily be bent, broken, or amended if the player is good enough.

In the elite athletic culture, there is no order and but one rule: win at any cost. The question is whether that cost has become too high.

While this book is not specifically about sports' societal impact, there is no question that American education's failed experiment with elite athletics has contributed to our All-American Addiction. While much of what transpires in high school and college athletics is positive, the problem remains that our country has lost perspective regarding the role of organized sport in our culture. We have come to glorify athletic accomplishment far more than academic achievement. And our high schools and, in particular, our colleges and universities, have, in large part, been responsible for allowing this culture to evolve.

The fact is that in the case of the cultural area of athletics, higher education has failed in its public mission by not providing the necessary leadership in establishing a healthy societal attitude regarding athletics. If a cultural consensus regarding the proper relationship between sport and education is ever going to be restored, it is up to the higher education community to initiate the process. Perhaps this is an unfair burden. After all, professional sports bear some responsibility. In an ideal world, perhaps they would. But the fact is, there is little incentive for professional sports organizations to initiate meaningful reform of the current system.

Thus, the question, not only for educational leaders but for our citizenry as well, is as follows: Are our educational and public health interests best served by the current system of elite athletics in America? At issue is not the value of elite athletics in our culture, but whether our educational institutions should be saddled with the responsibility of developing our future professional athletes. There is a way to structure the sports enterprise to enable it to more effectively meet the educational and public health needs of America. To find that model, all we have to do is look to Europe.

ENVISIONING A DIFFERENT FUTURE

Progress is impossible without change: and those who cannot change their minds can not change anything.

—George Bernard Shaw

Athletes often use a technique called "visualization" to improve their chances of success. For example, the athlete imagines an act such as hitting a baseball or envisions reacting during a competitive situation. It is believed that if the athlete sees herself performing a particular skill, it will improve her chances of actually performing that skill successfully. In other words, to achieve success, one must be able to visualize what success will look like.

The purpose of this chapter is to encourage the reader to envision success of another sort: the successful transformation of the role that athletics plays in our high schools, colleges, and culture. I am not talking about change around the fringes but a systemic change. A progressive vision of change from the current elite model of sports in America, where the vast majority of resources are heaped upon the few who show extraordinary potential, to one that would have as its fundamental purposes to use athletics as a tool to supplement the educational development of participants, to support the missions of our educational institutions, and to promote broad-based participation in activities that can be practiced for a lifetime for purposes of public health.

In such a model, the responsibility for the development of elite athletes and teams would shift from our educational institutions to private sports clubs and professional teams. Once a youngster is identified as having the potential to compete at an advanced athletic level, he or she would simply pursue that endeavor with a local club or professional team. This model works well throughout the rest of the world. In fact, the United States is the only country in the world in which elite athletes and teams are sponsored by high schools and colleges rather than local clubs and professional teams.

This vision is not about whether elite athletics are good or bad but whether the current system is best suited for making the most of athletics' potential to meet our nation's education and public health needs. There is a place for elite athletics in our culture. The question is simply whether that place should be in our schools.

A BETTER SYSTEM

Elite sport is an important American cultural institution. As such, its impact on our schools, communities, and culture must be critically assessed by us as individuals and, collectively, as a society. This is no different from what we must do for other American institutions. From our health care system to our welfare system, old ideas, programs, institutions, and philosophies must continually be examined, refined, and, if appropriate, restructured. And the fundamental standard of evaluation should be utility. Do these institutions continue to serve the public in relevant and timely ways? If it is determined, through honest debate and data-based research, that elite athletics have a positive impact on academic values and educational institutions, we should invest more heavily in them. But if elite athletics' supposed positive benefits are disproved, we have an obligation to reconsider that investment. To do anything else would be irresponsible.

One only needs to look in any newspaper's sports pages, watch the local television newscast, or tune in to ESPN's twenty-four-hour-a-day sports coverage to appreciate sports' popularity and the breadth of its influence in America. There is also no denying that virtually every aspect of the sports enterprise has changed over the past two decades. There is more money, more media exposure, more pressure to win, and that pressure is creeping further and further down the sport food chain. Regardless of how popular sports are, there are serious questions about the ways they have come to influence our lives, families, communities, and culture.

We have discussed how the current elite model of athletics undermines academic values and educational institutions. This impact is significant because our high schools and colleges exert tremendous influence over many aspects of American society, including public health, the educational preparedness of our workforce, civic spending priorities, and other elements of our civil society. In short, what transpires in our high school and university athletics programs is an issue of vital national interest. Thus, when we speak of athletics reform, whether at the youth, high school, or college level, the core issues are no longer simply the traditional fare of athlete welfare, academic integrity, performance enhancing drugs, overzealous parents, and presidential control of college programs. Today, reform is about the cultural values we will pass on to our children and grandchildren. It is about ensuring that we prize and reinforce values such as honesty, intelligence, and civility over athletic prowess. It is about the role of our educational institutions in promoting academic excellence, ensuring health and fitness, teaching our children, and, in the process, providing an example for all to emulate.

We have invested heavily in organized, elite athletics. Thus, it is imperative that we honestly evaluate how effectively the athletic enterprise is meeting the goals upon which it has been based. Simply because athletics is tremendously popular does not exempt it from community and educational standards of accountability. The question is whether our nation's system of organized athletics, as currently constructed, is meeting its educational, civic, and public health purposes.

Sadly, the answer is that it is not. It is within our educational system that this shortfall has had the most impact and greatest consequences. Despite how much we love our high school and college sports, we must be honest about their impact on our culture. It is time to acknowledge that American education's experiment with elite athletics has been a failure.

Before continuing, I would like to be clear on two points. First, I love sports. I love playing them. I love watching them. I believe they play an important role in our lives. I do not advocate the elimination of organized sports in America. This is neither wise nor realistic. It is critical, however, that we honestly evaluate their impact on our culture and, if appropriate, restructure our educational investment in athletics accordingly.

The issue is balance and perspective, not elimination. Sports' potential to positively contribute to our society is enormous. If kept in the proper perspective, sports provide compelling entertainment, contribute to a healthy lifestyle, and build character in participants. The problem, however, is that as a society we have lost perspective regarding the role that organized athletics should play in our culture. And our educational institutions have played a significant role in that development.

Second, the type of athletics to which I refer are elite, interscholastic and intercollegiate sports. There is absolutely no doubt that athletics have a place within our educational institutions. Athletic activities can and should be utilized to supplement the educational experience of participants as well as the academic mission of the institution. And there is a place for elite athletics within American culture. The question is whether that place should be in our educational system. In short, should our educational institutions be saddled with the responsibility of developing elite athletes and teams? And is our current system of athletics the best model for meeting our nation's educational and public health needs?

The answer is no. But if our current system is not the best model, what is?

The European club-sport model is.

A BETTER SYSTEM

It is notable that the United States is the only country in the world in which elite athletics programs are sponsored by high schools and universities. In Europe, the responsibility for the development of elite athletes and teams is borne by private sports clubs or professional teams. Could it be that, in the case of the development and promotion of highly competitive, elite athletics, the Europeans, rather than we Americans, have it right?

In Europe, when a youngster is identified as having superior talent and potential for a particular sport, he or she pursues that sport through a local club program. The responsibility of the educational system regarding athletics is to promote and encourage broad-based participation in activities that can be enjoyed for a lifetime for purposes of improving public health. This, stands in contrast to the American system, which devours increasingly large amounts of resources for an activity that has as its primary purpose providing public entertainment and serving the athletic needs of a select group of athletes. These purposes are achieved at the expense of the athlete's academic development and the host institution's academic mission.

While the move to the European club-sport system may sound radical, it is not. Our school systems and universities would survive without highly competitive sports, as would our elite athletes and coaches. Local organizations and youth groups would develop and sponsor more comprehensive athletic programs. And, as in Europe, existing professional teams would begin to sponsor their own feeder systems and programs. Each professional league would be forced to develop a minor league system, similar to the one that currently exists in baseball. In short, the responsibility for developing future professional athletes would shift from our high schools and colleges to private sports clubs and professional teams. In such a system, "there is no controversy about what to call them. They are neither student-athletes nor athlete-students. They are students *and* athletes. The spheres of activity are separate and distinct" (Putnam, 1999, p. 212).

In some sports, such a shift is well on its way. Many elite athletes in the sports of soccer, basketball, and swimming have come to consider their participation on elite local clubs or traveling Amateur Athletic Union or all-star teams more important than participation on their high school teams. To these athletes, this is a logical progression of their involvement in youth sports clubs and elite travel teams. And, as mentioned, the direct link between high school athletics and the educational institution has become increasingly tenuous as a growing number of high school coaches are not professional teachers. These trends are simply the first signs that the decoupling of elite athletics and high schools is under way.

Shifting the responsibility for conducting elite sports programs from our nation's schools and colleges to outside sports clubs is clearly in the best interests of our schools, athletes, and coaches. Our educational system would be rid of a highly visible source of hypocrisy and scandal. Intramural, physical education, and wellness programs could be expanded, resulting in more students being able to avail themselves of health- and exercise-related resources. The credibility of our educational system would grow because such a change would signify that our schools and communities have strong educational values and public health priorities. With such a change, our educational system would be better positioned to serve the broad, long-term, health and exercise needs of America.

It is interesting to note that American students fare poorly academically when compared to students in countries such as Japan, Germany, France, and South Korea, to name only a few. Students from these and most other industrialized nations consistently perform better than American students in science and math. American students also consistently rate last in the area of physical fitness. Although there is no data demonstrating a direct link between these two dubious distinctions, the fact that America is the only country where schools are responsible for the development of elite athletes and teams leads one to think that there has to be a correlation.

EMBRACING POSITIVE CHANGE

Contrary to what avid sports fans might believe, our nation's educational system would not collapse if the responsibility for developing elite athletes and teams were "privatized." While our school systems might be less dynamic, and in some ways less fun without elite athletics, they will continue to go about the business of educating. In fact, the education of students would likely improve with the elimination of such programs as the focus on academics would intensify.

Athletes and coaches would continue to have the opportunity to hone their skills as elite sports activities and training would simply shift to other local sponsoring agencies. As in Europe, local sports organizations would develop and sponsor more comprehensive athletics programs, and professional teams would sponsor feeder systems and programs.

Critics of such change will cite research indicating a positive correlation between various academic, health, and social indicators and involvement in high school athletics. While such evidence can be convincing, it begs a larger question. If we believe so strongly in the educational and community-building value of athletics participation, why do we have a system that weeds out kids at younger and younger ages? If children learn so much from participation in athletics, shouldn't the system be designed to involve everyone? Just as all children need to learn a certain set of math, reading, and science skills to have a chance at a successful life, so too in the case of having a healthy life. A healthy lifestyle does not just happen. Lifelong fitness principles must be taught, nurtured, and practiced to become an ongoing part of an individual's lifestyle. Unfortunately, our current elite system of interscholastic and intercollegiate athletics eats up the vast majority of sports-related school extracurricular resources. The result is that our schools have few resources to apply to the goal of teaching our children to develop a lifelong commitment to staying active and physically fit.

Further, we must ask whether these positive correlations exist because of involvement with a high school team or simply any team, regardless of the sponsoring agency? Could it be that athletes who achieve academically do so because they are high achievers, no matter what the endeavor? If this were the case, these young people would perform well academically, regardless of whether their team was sponsored by the high school or a local club organization.

In short, there is nothing to suggest that athletics programs must be a part of an educational institution for young people to learn from coaches the lessons of discipline, sportsmanship, teamwork, and sacrifice. The potential to utilize athletics as a means to build character and teach these lessons will remain, regardless of the team's sponsoring agency.

This is not to say that college athletics needs to go back to "the good old days," those glory days of a supposed innocence and simpler sports existence. You can not turn back the clock. Those days are gone, if they ever existed in the first place. That said, there is no reason to surrender to current forces and abandon what were supposed to be the founding principles and core values of athletics programs sponsored by educational institutions: that athletes are not a separate and distinct class of students but rather representative of the general student body and that the purpose of athletics is to supplement and support the educational process of young people and the mission of the institution. High school and college athletics were designed to be extracurricular activities. Students were never intended to be engaged in athletics as a full-time job. Nor were our educational institutions ever intended to be in the business of operating professional sports franchises.

Obviously, community resistance to such a shift would be enormous. The history and culture of high school sports is very deep and extremely powerful. That said, the distance between cheering for your local high school football team and a town team consisting of essentially the same group of athletes is not as great as it appears. The driving force that fuels the passion for a local team is not necessarily high school pride but rather community pride. "The team is a community enterprise, and its successes are shared by the community, its losses mourned in concert" (Coleman, 1961, p. 42). The high school team is simply the vehicle through which that community pride is currently expressed.

As Miracle and Rees write in *Lessons of the Locker Room: The Myth of School Sports* (1994), "If you think football is important and you support your school's team, and if our team beats your team, then our school beats your school, our community beats your community. . . . It is not surprising, then, that communities are less interested in what high school sports does for the participants and more interested in what it does for the fans" (p. 158).

After an initial outcry from those who do not appreciate the purpose of our nation's educational institutions, it is quite possible that fans would come to identify with the team of their choice, despite the sponsor being a local car dealership rather than the high school. Supporters of the school would simply display their spirit by supporting other activities, such as music or theater groups. Thus, it is debatable whether a significant decline in interest in the community's football team would result simply because the name on the front of the jersey bore the name of the town rather than the town's high school.

Miracle and Rees (1994) consider one argument for eliminating competitive sports in this way:

> One reaction to debunking the myth of high school sport is to say that sports are educationally worthless and should be eradicated from high schools. Although we reject that line of action, it is not unprecedented. Obviously, there can be education without sport. For example, some European countries such as Germany have no interscholastic athletics. In fact, there is some validity to the argument that schools without sports would help to focus the energies and commitment of students, educators and community members on the primary reason for schools—academics. There is no doubt that some individuals from time to time forget that schools are really meant to be about reading, writing, mathematics, science, social studies, languages, literature, and the humanities. Today, it is becoming difficult to see how sports fits into the curriculum. Moreover, without historical perspective, it is difficult to understand why sport was ever introduced to American schools and rationalized on the basis of academic relevance.
>
> Without sport, high schools would continue to operate much as they have for most students since desegregation in the 1960's. Students would go to school each day, attend class, grumble about homework, hang out with their friends, flirt with other students, and have fun. The difference would be that they would have to organize their social life around activities other than athletic contests. (pp. 203–04)

Regardless of the outcry and resistance, we must critically assess our nation's educational priorities and outcomes, including elite athletics and its tremendous influence on those priorities and outcomes. Ultimately, American education must structure itself according to what will best enable it to meet its responsibility to meet the educational and public health needs of our children.

CHANGE ON CAMPUS

The argument for moving elite athletics from our college campuses to the club system presents a different challenge, requiring the unraveling of a series of myths and long held assumptions that have thwarted any serious challenge to college athletics' status quo. The interplay between and among these beliefs and assumptions is very complex. Much of the rest of this book will be spent addressing the arguments, myths, and assumptions that have long served as barriers to progressive reform of sports in our schools, colleges, and culture.

The first of those misguided assumptions is that college athletics will never be significantly reformed because it has become so ingrained in the fabric of not only higher education but of our society. The public has come to expect that our colleges and universities provide exciting and compelling entertainment in the form of athletics. This is viewed as a service that American higher education provides the public. Compounding the myth is the fact that athletics serves a valuable function for the university as a rallying point as well as an effective activity around which to raise funds and conduct university events. These notions have fueled the widespread belief that reform is unlikely because athletics is simply too important to both the individual college or university and the public for it to be altered in any significant way. The concern is that altering the "product" in a way that might result in a lower "quality of game" would then result in diminished public appeal. This fear is unfounded for reasons that will be articulated in chapter 6.

It is the fear of diminishing college athletics' public appeal that has served as a major barrier to the meaningful reform of the current system. As a result, the focus of athletics reform has been to address the symptoms of the problem, not the root cause. Traditionally, the college athletics reform debate has centered on academics, with concerns regarding financial excesses and overcommercialization emerging more recently. These problems, however, are symptoms rather than the root cause of college athletics' ills.

It has long been thought that raising academic standards for athletics eligibility is the surest way to integrate athletes into the student body and athletics programs into the campus community. Unfortunately, raising academic standards has had only marginal impact on the conduct of athletics programs. As mentioned, 2003 and 2004 represented a particularly dark period of athletics' excess, with multiple incidents of institutions engaging in academic fraud and recruiting abuses. And while graduation rates of athletes have risen since 1986, this rise mirrors the rise in graduation rates of the general student body.

Even a recent NCAA initiative to hold coaches and teams more accountable academically will likely have minimal impact. Touted as the "incentives/disincentives" plan, it is designed to punish teams and institutions by withholding scholarships, money, and, eventually, access to NCAA tournaments if the academic performance of athletes is substandard. To date, the only individual who pays a real price for academic failure has been the athlete. While it is significant that, for the first time, coach and institutional accountability are being considered, to think that this is a cure-all is misguided.

It is precisely because coaches and programs will now be directly impacted that the propensity to cheat will increase. While a team or coach is impacted to a degree when an athlete flunks out of school, the team and the coach move on, relatively unscathed. When coaches and programs are directly impacted by the loss of scholarships or a ban from postseason play when athletes do not perform academically, the stakes for keeping them eligible, whatever the cost, rises considerably.

The fact is more academic reform will not fundamentally alter the Division I landscape. Raising academic standards does not mainstream athletes. Rather, these changes result in a higher bar for academic fraud, greater dependence on athletics department tutoring services, the creation of pseudo-majors to keep athletes eligible, and an arms race in the area of academic support programs and facilities. Attempting to reform college athletics by raising academic standards is like trying to fit a round peg into a square hole. No matter how high academic standards are raised, athletes with little interest in being a part of the regular student body or athletes who arrive on campus significantly underprepared academically will never fit comfortably into the academic community.

Efforts to reform the fiscal excesses of major college athletics have similarly failed. The most obvious example of this failure occurred at the 1992 NCAA Cost Reduction Convention. After a full year of debate, dialogue, and review of various proposals, the NCAA membership produced virtually nothing to address the issue of rising costs. Today, the athletics arms race continues as the number of schools losing money on athletics grows, as does the average athletics department deficit. As with academics, rising costs are merely a symptom of the root cause.

Most recently, a third reform theme has emerged: that the excessive commercialism surrounding major college athletics programs is eroding academic values and institutional integrity. Again, this is a myth. As will be explained in chapter 6, concentrating on the rampant commercialism of college athletics misses the higher education forest for the athletic trees.

THE ROOT CAUSE

It is time to acknowledge that academically underprepared athletes, low graduation rates, financial excesses, and commercial and corporate influences are only symptoms of American higher education's failed experiment with elite athletics. Rather, it is the model that American higher education has chosen to use in reaping the commercial potential of athletics that is the problem. It is the misguided attempt to perpetuate this model that has resulted in the failure to address, in any meaningful way, these symptoms. It is no longer in doubt that Division I athletics, in particular football and basketball, with other sports marching down the same road, have become very expensive professional teams in college uniforms. And the responsibility for the evolution of that model lies not in corporate boardrooms but solely at the feet of American higher education.

For the past century, American higher education has rushed headlong down the road of making athletics bigger, better, and more professional. Division I athletics have come to look, feel, and operate so much like the pros that there is very little to distinguish the values and operating principles of the two. Regrettably, that road has taken athletics to a point where they have become widely viewed as promoting values and practices that actually run counter to those of the academic community. The competitive pressure to increase athletics department budgets has resulted in an arms race that threatens the fiscal integrity of a growing number of institutions, forces individuals and institutions to compromise academic integrity, and promotes the embrace of commercial principles and partnerships that undermine institutional priorities.

The failure of Division I to contribute in timely, relevant, and fiscally sound ways to the educational missions of our universities is not a result of excessive commercialism or low graduation rates. Rather, it is the fact that the higher education community has allowed the professional sports model to develop on campus virtually unchecked. Higher education simply has no business being in the business of professional athletics. Thus, it is time for Division I athletics to take a new road. Specifically, the professional model of intercollegiate athletics must be dismantled and rebuilt, not as a mirror of professional sports but in the image of an educational institution.

At a time when college athletics has reached unprecedented levels of commercial popularity, how can it be said that its incorporation into higher education has failed? Perhaps a better way to pose the question is as follows: If higher education's experiment with professional athletics has been so successful, why is it that virtually all of the commercial justifications for the professional model are not being realized? As outlined in chapter 1, the vast majority of programs lose money and do not have nearly as positive an impact on enrollment, fundraising, and public relations as we have long believed.

Further, in many areas, the professional model of sports is having an increasingly negative impact on campus culture. The level of intensity of everything connected to the athletics experience, from recruiting to individual commitment to the sport to the level of play, has increased at all levels of sport, from peewee to professional leagues, all driven by the increasingly professionalized nature of the entire sports system. The result is that the chasm between athletics values ánd priorities and those of the academic community, always apparent, is becoming greater.

More important, however, is how the evolution of the professional model of athletics has contributed to a fundamental disconnect between athletics department performance standards and educational priorities and mission. NCAA president Myles Brand referred to this disconnect in his 2004 "State of the Association Address":

> Generally, the changes in the Collegiate Model have been rather subtle, the result of success, in most cases, and the inevitable desire for more success. But as benign as these changes appeared at the time, the cumulative effect is an erosion of the bond between athletics and academics. The mission of the universities is education, broadly understood, and college sports must serve that mission. Intercollegiate athletics is not a freestanding, wholly autonomous enterprise that

is located in close proximity to a university. To the degree that athletic programs look and behave like such freestanding enterprises, we have seen the type of drift toward the Professional Model that will diminish and in the long run will eliminate the value of the program to its university.

As mentioned, athletics was formally incorporated into higher education because it was believed it could be used to contribute to institutional mission by attracting resources and advancing educational ideals. That being the case, it would follow that the "success" of such programs would be judged by how effective they are in meeting those goals. Unfortunately, the justifications upon which higher education accepted athletics are not the standards upon which we have come to judge them. Today, a college athletic program's "success" is measured by wins and losses, revenue generated, television appearances, and championship banners hung from gymnasium rafters. Such standards have little relevance as they relate to the societal challenges that higher education is expected to provide leadership in addressing. Rather, these are the standards that are used to measure the success of professional sports franchises.

Consider the essence of professional athletics: pay for play. Despite the idealist rhetoric of the athletics establishment, the reality is that the contract between the athlete and the institution no longer represents the ideal of scholarship (pay) for education. It is not pay for education when it is plain to everyone—coaches, fans, faculty, media, and, especially, the athletes—that they are on campus, first and foremost, to play ball. *That*, by any definition, is pay for play.

The professional model is also about paying whatever you have to for coaches, staff, facilities, scouting, travel, and anything else that coaches believe might make the difference between winning and losing, regardless of how outrageous or remote the actual impact. This culture of spending has escalated to an absurd level to where it makes neither fiscal nor educational sense. Professional sports is also about playing anywhere at anytime to reap television revenues. And professional athletics is about the expectation that athletes train year round and sacrifice not only their academic and social dreams and aspirations for "The Program" but their bodies as well. Division I athletics has evolved to a point where it has come to mirror these aspects of the professional model.

While one of higher education's strengths is its tremendous diversity of services, programs, opportunities, and mission, it is time to face the fact that, in the case of athletics, higher education may not be able to have it all. Specifically, the sponsorship of highly competitive, professionalized, elite athletics—in other words, the professional model of athletics—should be left to the professional leagues. The history of American higher education offers many examples of programs or departments that were downsized or eliminated when it became apparent that they had become obsolete, failed to meet their purpose, or become a drain on institutional resources. It is time for colleges and universities to eliminate their departments of professional athletics.

BREAKING THE CHAIN

This is not to say, however, that elimination of the professional model of college athletics will result in the removal of intercollegiate athletics from higher education or the elimination of the NCAA. College athletics is too steeped in tradition and its structure too established to allow such a dramatic shift to occur. Athletics has become so ingrained in the campus culture and such an important vehicle for larger university purposes that the complete elimination of intercollegiate athletics of all kinds would not be in the best interests of American higher education.

It is important to note the difference in the prescriptions for change in the current elite model of athletics in high schools versus colleges. In the case of interscholastic sports, the adoption of the European model will result in the removal of elite sports from the high school. This shift will allow our secondary schools to utilize athletics activities in ways that will better serve community education and public health needs. This will occur through increased emphasis on programs in physical education, intramural and wellness programs designed to encourage broad-based participation for purposes of public health. The entertainment and community-building function of sports would simply shift to local or regional club teams.

In the case of higher education, the elimination of departments of professional athletics will have little impact on the entertainment and commercial functions of the athletics department. After a period of adjustment, much of what the public sees will remain relatively unchanged. What will be dramatically different is that the focus of the enterprise will be education rather than professional athletics. As NCAA president Myles Brand often says, the elimination of the professional model of college athletics will result, not in the elimination of athletics, but rather in "turning down their volume." College athletics will continue to provide an entertainment service but it will be provided with real students who are engaged in a legitimate educational experience guided by coaches who are true educators rather than professional athletes paid to perform athletically for what has become a professional sports franchise. Those athletes who wish to invest in the professional model can continue to pursue that goal with a local club or professional team.

While these approaches to resolving American education's failed experiment with elite athletics are different, they are linked. As mentioned, what we do in our college athletics programs, the values we embrace, the messages we send, and the examples we set filter down to all levels of sport. The public looks to higher education to provide educational leadership, including the role and purpose of sport in our communities and educational institutions. The higher education community must come together to meet that leadership responsibility by dismantling the destructive system, ideals, and philosophy of professional athletics that is undermining academic values and educational priorities at all levels of our society.

Regardless of the impression one might get from the bare-chested, face-painted rabid fan, ultimately, it is far more important that our colleges and universities develop scholars, advance knowledge, and produce important research than train future professional athletes and field elite sports teams. While the public firestorm over such a change would be monumental, with time the public would come to accept the change and our educational institutions would go on about their business of educating our populace.

American higher education is at an important crossroads regarding athletics. This may be the last opportunity for significant reform; the last chance to tame the ever growing beast that is college athletics. In short, the clock is running out on college athletics reform. Despite a growing gap between the athletics and academic cultures on campus, fear of vast public and alumni outcry leaves educational leaders with little stomach to take on such an explosive issue. Thus, the prevailing notion is that systemic change is not possible. If universities continue to sponsor a professional athletic model that has virtually nothing in common with the values and purposes of an academic institution, the day will come when higher education leaders will lose their credibility and ability to implement any change. That change will be forced from outside academe, most likely from Congress.

As more money flows into the enterprise, as commercialism increases, as the win-at-all-costs culture grows, and as March Madness marches on, the forces working against reform are enormous. But if the reformers prevail, seemingly against all odds, the impact would be monumental and inspirational. If the higher education community can reject the professional model of sports and all that it stands for, it will serve as an extremely potent example demonstrating that reform of high school, youth, and community sports is not simply a pipe dream but a real possibility.

But will college athletics change? Can it be reformed in more than just a superficial way?

Most say this is doubtful. Some say, it is impossible. I disagree. The opportunity to realize the vision outlined above has never been greater. As will be discussed in the following pages, never before have the fields upon which the seeds of reform must be sown been more fertile.

A CHANGED CONTEXT FOR REFORM

I beg your pardon, I didn't recognize
you—I've changed a lot.

—Oscar Wilde

History provides many examples of monumental societal and cultural change. Empires have risen and fallen. Dynasties have collapsed or been conquered. Governments have been overthrown. Ideologies have waxed and waned. Why is it, then, that we find it so hard to envision systemic change in the way elite athletics is conducted in America?

Granted, the forces against fundamental structural and cultural change in America's system of athletics are very strong. College athletics, for example, is an enterprise that has grown virtually unchecked for over one hundred years. Universities were competing athletically for more than sixty years before the first attempt to regulate anything other than the specific playing rules of the game. As public interest in, media coverage of, and the financial stakes surrounding college athletics have escalated, they have come to assume an enormous presence and influence in our culture. The enterprise has grown in every sense—bigger crowds, more money, greater visibility, and more television and media coverage. As a result, there is more pressure to win. Like a freight train careening down the tracks, accelerating and gathering more power, college athletics has generated a massive amount of energy and inertia. With more lucrative television contracts, never-ending media coverage, bigger-than-life coaches, and a sports-crazed populace that seems to be unable to get enough of that speeding train, no wonder many believe it is impossible to reform college athletics.

Periodic attempts at athletics reform are almost as much a part of the higher education landscape as the classroom lecture. Like clockwork, every fifteen or twenty years, a series of scandals leads to public outrage and a subsequent national reform initiative. In 1906, the NCAA was formed as a result of calls from President Theodore Roosevelt to reform the violent nature of football. In 1929, the Carnegie Commission for the Advancement of Teaching released a comprehensive study of athletics that revealed rampant professionalism and commercialization. In 1946, the NCAA adopted the Principles for the Conduct of Intercollegiate Athletics. This measure, referred to as the "Sanity Code," not only placed limits on the amount and types of financial aid an athlete could receive but, for the first time, also established a mechanism to enforce those rules. In 1952, the NCAA Convention voted to establish an NCAA Membership Committee to consider complaints of failure to comply with the rules or its constitution and adopted regulatory legislation governing the administration of financial aid to athletes. Also in that year, an American

Council on Education (ACE) report called for more stringent eligibility rules, basing financial awards to athletes on academic achievement and economic need and prohibiting freshman eligibility. More recently, there have been what many consider a series of short periods of reform, starting with the establishment of the NCAA Presidents Commission in 1984 and the release of two reports from the Knight Commission on Intercollegiate Athletics in 1991 and a decade later in 2001.

My purpose is not to dismiss these reform efforts. In some cases, they have resulted in real change. For example, the formation of the NCAA in 1906 was an enormous step in making the game of football safer. And the adoption of the Sanity Code began to place much needed restrictions on the recruiting process. Typically, however, the reform scenario plays out as follows. A series of scandals ignites widespread public indignation over the excesses of big-time athletics. Calls for sweeping reform are heard from many quarters. A commission full of high-profile educational leaders is formed to examine the problems and recommend reform measures. A series of changes are proposed, some of which, if implemented, have little long-lasting impact. Amid much self-congratulatory praise, the public is once again appeased. And life within our college athletics departments returns to business as usual until the next series of scandals reignites the process.

Despite the fact that attempts to implement meaningful, long-lasting reform have recurred periodically, the growth and negative impact of professionalized college athletics on not only institutional integrity and academic values but also our society continues. The three-hundred-pound

gorilla lurking in the corner of the higher education classroom continues to grow, gobbling up resources, energy,
attention, credibility, and emotion, while spreading its
influence to the high school, junior high school, and peewee league levels. Like a cancer, it continues to infect its
host. As stated in the "Letter of Transmittal" in the 2001
Knight Commission report, "We find that the problems
of big-time college sports have grown rather than diminished" (Knight Foundation Commission on Intercollegiate
Athletics, 2001a, p. 4).

All of this, however, may be about to change. For the
first time in the history of American higher education, the
table of reform may finally be fully set. Despite a recent
rash of scandals that has led many to suggest that reform
is a lost cause, a more accurate analogy for the current state
of college athletics is that of the night always being dark-
est before the first light of dawn. Upon closer examination,
there are many signs suggesting that we may finally be
approaching the tipping point for revolutionary change.

The possibilities of a new dawn exist because there are
two key reform influences that have changed dramatically.
The first, which will be explained in this chapter, relates to
the fact that the context within which today's reform efforts
are being played out has changed dramatically over the past
twenty-five years. And the second, which will be addressed
in the following chapter, is the building and establishment
of a long-term, far-reaching reform movement.

In short, to think that over one hundred years of virtually
unchecked growth will be slowed, stopped, and reversed by
periodic reform efforts, a one-time commission, or a special
report is naïve. Reform of such a powerful force requires a

long-term, sustained movement, driven by a critical mass of committed people and organizations with ample resolve, coming together to push back against that force.

To achieve systemic reform of an institution such as big-time college athletics requires a change in the many external and cultural forces that influence the enterprise. In other words, change occurs with and is influenced by a larger cultural context. These different sets of change agents form a symbiotic relationship that evolves into something bigger than the sum of its parts, generating the momentum to drive meaningful change.

This is not to say that some of the contextual factors that will be identified were not in place during previous reform efforts. For example, there have been other periods when higher education has faced a challenging economic climate. It was believed that the economic straits higher education faced in the 1930s would spur the type of reform suggested in the 1929 Carnegie Report. But a dire economic climate, of itself, is not sufficient to influence systemic change. Change of the magnitude advocated in these pages will not occur in the wake of one or two changed contextual factors but requires a confluence of many factors.

The American Civil Rights movement provides an example. Individual acts of people such as Rosa Parks, Thurgood Marshall, and Martin Luther King or specific events such as the murder of Medgar Evers did not, in and of themselves, drive sweeping cultural change. While they may have provided individual sparks to the Civil Rights movement, those sparks would not have caught fire and spread had not broad sociological changes occurred that made the soil for civil rights change more fertile. For example, the distinction with which blacks served in the army in World War II greatly changed the context against which these individual actions played out after the war. Their service in the war forever changed, for a large number of people, the way blacks are perceived and accepted within America. When these soldiers returned home, the cultural context within which the Civil Rights movement was being played out had changed dramatically. In short, if Rosa Parks had refused to move to the back of the bus in 1920, her fate would have been much different.

Today, there are many signs that the necessary ingredients to drive systemic change of college athletics are coalescing. Many of the factors that have prevented meaningful reform in the past have, for various reasons, changed—in some cases, rather dramatically. The result is that we may finally be on the verge of the intersection of a critical mass of people, institutions, and ideas with the series of changing cultural and contextual factors needed to transform the role of sports in our educational institutions and in our society. Consider, for example, the following contextual factors that have changed in ways that make progressive, systemic change more possible.

LONG-TERM RESOLVE AND ENGAGEMENT OF COLLEGE PRESIDENTS

Malcolm Gladwell, author of *The Tipping Point: How Little Things Can Make a Big Difference* (2000), maintains that there are three factors that lead to a tipping point at which fundamental, broad-based cultural change occurs.

Such change is spurred by the efforts of a handful of exceptional, influential people. Gladwell refers to this factor as the "Law of the Few," where a tiny percentage of people can have influence or drive widespread cultural change. Further, the *nature* of the messenger is also critical. There have been many individuals or small groups of higher education stakeholders who have, through the years, called for athletics reform. For example, faculty members have long been uncomfortable with the impact of athletics programs on academe, with individual members expressing concerns. However, there is a difference between a faculty member, a group of faculty, or the random sports reformer or reform organization calling for change and a group of college presidents becoming engaged in the issue.

Despite the fact that it has been long known that presidents hold the key to reform, it was not until the formation of the NCAA Presidents Commission in 1984 that they began to exert that influence seriously. For example, the 1929 Carnegie Report emphatically stated that presidents must lead the reform effort. Yet, as late as 1954, the NCAA Convention reaffirmed the long-standing principle of faulty control as the first step in any regulatory process. In short, meaningful and functional presidential authority and control is a relatively new phenomenon.

This does not, however, mean that presidents alone are responsible for athletics reform. Rather, presidents are the best equipped to plant the seeds of reform and nurture them to fruition. But, as with any crop, it takes time and attention to reap a harvest. Before cultural change of the magnitude necessary to reform college athletics can occur, not only must a core of influential leaders develop the resolve and commitment to change it, but that resolve must be sustained over a long period of time.

Prior to the explosion of television and media coverage of college athletics that began in earnest with the rise of ESPN in the early and mid 1980s, college athletics, while certainly important to a university, were not nearly as visible, influential, and pervasive a cultural force as they are today. Presidents viewed athletics as important but not deserving of a significant amount of their attention. But as visibility increased, budgets soared, and athletics scandals exploded, presidents came to the realization that athletics had grown to have a significant impact on the institution.

With the formation of the NCAA Presidents Commission in 1984, presidents began to address the issue of athletics reform with the commitment and resolve necessary to endure what would be a long-term fight. Presidents have since been consistently engaged in various reform initiatives. These specific measures will be listed in the following chapter. The point, however, is that, despite the belief that presidents would not remain engaged in the reform battle, they have, in fact, remained so for almost twenty-five years.

ABSENCE OF A PROCESS TO INITIATE CHANGE

College presidents, no matter how influential, are unable to initiate substantive change without an established process through which they can formally and systematically implement and enact reform principles and programs. While noble and well intentioned, previous reform efforts had little chance of succeeding because the administrative and governance structure necessary to implement change was not in place. It was not until the NCAA Presidents Commission was formed that a formal vehicle and structure through which presidents could effectively wield their influence began to take shape. While the specific procedures, policies, and actions that created the foundation necessary to support and facilitate change will be outlined in the following chapter, the establishment of a legislative process and governance structure through which presidents could effectively exert their oversight authority and initiate meaningful change did not begin to develop until the mid to late 1980s.

LACK OF EVIDENCE

For over one hundred years, institutions have been making decisions, establishing policy, and investing in athletics based on a series of assumptions that have come to be accepted as gospel, despite the fact that there has been little, if any, evidence to support them. These assumptions have been perpetuated and passed from generation to generation of coaches, administrators, media, athletes, and fans without their authenticity being seriously challenged. As a result, they have come to be accepted as enduring, unassailable truths.

While there has always been a sense of the real and potential problems inherent in an educational institutional sponsoring highly competitive athletics, only recently have we begun to fully understand those negative impacts. This new understanding is the result of an increasing amount of research and data that has quantified athletics' negative impact and placed into serious question the validity of their benefits or disproved those benefits outright.

For example, the ideas that athletics programs make money for their institutions, that winning teams have a positive impact on institutional giving, and that athletics participation builds character have, for the most part, been revealed as myths. While it certainly seems possible, and indeed logical, that such assumptions would be true, the fact is that, in an increasing number of cases, they are not.

Much evidence to support these myth-breaking assertions was generated by the research that served as the basis for a book by James Shulman and William Bowen entitled *The Game of Life: College Sports and Educational Values*. Released in 2001, the authors analyzed data on ninety thousand students who attended colleges and universities in the 1950s, 1970s, and 1990s. The book has had a tremendous impact on the dialogue regarding the role and influence of athletics on campus, not simply because it challenges many of the heretofore sacred myths surrounding intercollegiate athletics, but because its myth-breaking assertions are backed by a significant amount of research. An argument or theory is much more persuasive when it is backed up by solid data. The result is that it has become more difficult to promote many of the long-held claims of benefits attributed to college athletics when a growing body of research indicates that they are not true.

During past reform efforts, if the benefits of the sponsorship of intercollegiate athletics were challenged, the athletic establishment would simply rally around these myths, cite them as absolute truths, and claim that reform was unnecessary. Who was going to challenge the high-profile coach or athletics director on these assumptions? These were heroes, perched high on their pedestals, deified by the news media and fans. Suggestions for reform initiatives were often dismissed before any serious and open debate regarding them could occur. No one dared refute the "power coach," regardless of whether his claims were based on facts. Thus, the myths surrounding athletics prevailed, intensified, and became even more ingrained in our collective consciousness.

While questions regarding athletics' impact on academic values and institutional mission have existed since the first days of intercollegiate competition, the critical mass of data and empirical evidence needed to disprove many of the justifications and fundamental assumptions regarding the impact of elite athletics on participants, the institutions that sponsor them, and our society was simply not available during prior reform periods. This, however, is changing dramatically as researchers have been generating a growing body of information regarding that impact. All within the higher education community should welcome this new wave of research because it will provide academic and athletics leaders with a more complete body of information upon which to base decisions and establish policy.

LACK OF BROAD-BASED INVOLVEMENT

There have always been individuals who believe that big-time college athletics negatively impact academic values and educational institutions. Most of them, however, also believe that athletics' impact does not directly affect them. Therefore, they do not consider athletics to be a primary concern. Further, they believe that college sports are never going to change and that an individual can not do anything about it. So why get involved?

Faculty are probably most guilty of this attitude, as they have traditionally been more interested in teaching or pursuing their research interests than in getting involved in what many have seen as a hopeless crusade against athletics. College presidents also provide a good example of this attitude. Many have made the very practical decision not to put their job on the line by "taking on" athletics because they did not want to place other elements of their institutional agenda in jeopardy. Presidents have often come to the very reasoned decision that it is impossible to grow an institution's endowment, raise the academic profile of the student body, or position an institution for the future through a successful capital campaign if they get fired over athletics. Why should presidents risk being able to complete far more important components of their campuswide agendas or other educational goals due to a battle over athletics? In 1985, William Atchley provided a very visible example of the perils of making a stand over athletics while president of Clemson University. Atchley fired Danny Ford, a very popular football coach, and soon found himself out of a job.

Many faculty, academic administrators, and board members have long been uneasy with athletics' relationship to the institution. While sensing that athletics' impact on institutional values and academic integrity was not as positive as was commonly accepted, most did not make a direct connection between athletics department actions and influence and their jobs, lives, communities, or families. Thus, the motivation for a faculty member, trustee, coach, or academic administrator to devote much energy and commitment to championing or even participating in reform efforts was limited. Those who did make the connection and stepped forward to speak out were often marginalized, castigated, or run out of town.

One such case was that of Linda Bensel-Myers. While an English professor at the University of Tennessee, she blew the whistle on widespread academic fraud in the football program. As a result, she became an outcast on campus. She was ridiculed and threatened by fans, coaches, and athletics administrators and subjected to office break-ins and tapped phone lines. Most disappointingly, she was shunned by fellow faculty. Eventually, she accepted a similar position at the University of Denver. In the mid 1980s, Jan Kemp, an English professor at the University of Georgia, and, in the late 1990s, Jan Ganglehoff, an academic advisor at the University of Minnesota, suffered similar fates.

But as athletics has grown in influence and excess, it is becoming increasingly obvious that what transpires in the athletics department has impact far beyond the walls of campus stadiums and arenas. An athletics scandal impacts the integrity of the entire university. General university funds spent on athletics are funds that are not spent on attracting quality students and faculty and improving educational programs, research initiatives, or academic facilities. And the message sent when the highest paid university employee is the football or basketball coach is certainly not a positive academic message.

A 2003 report from the University of Florida's Lombardi Program on Measuring University Performance is simply the latest piece of evidence of athletics' impact on the broader university community. The report concludes that

> universities that succeed in the competition for research faculty and superior students invest a large portion of their financial base in attracting and retaining these superior faculty and students, and then invest even more in the acquisition of research grants, contracts, special student programs, and other quality-enhancing elements. We believe that the data presented in our previous reports demonstrates that the amount of discretionary university dollars invested in faculty, student and research competition is the critical element in successful competition for quality. It is likely, then, that university activities like intercollegiate athletics, which consume discretionary dollars without enhancing the university's academic competitive success, will inhibit the acquisition of quality. (p. 33)

There has also been a recent and very significant development that has greatly broadened the range of people and institutions actively engaged in the reform issue. As mentioned, the release of *The Game of Life* by Bowen and Shulman, as well as a follow-up book entitled *Reclaiming the Game: College Sports and Educational Values*, by Bowen and Sarah Levin, provided an enormous amount of data regarding the impact of athletics on academic values and institutional mission. Just as important, these books documented the widening gap between sport and education not only at Division I institutions but at virtually every institution sponsoring intercollegiate athletics, including Ivy League and selective liberal arts colleges. Apparently, what had been assumed to be a problem only at the big-time institutions of NCAA Division I-A is a myth.

While the abuses surrounding big-time college athletics were familiar, the effect of documenting athletics' increasingly negative impact on small universities has been enormous. These revelations have reconfigured the field upon which athletics reform will be played out. The implications for presidents, governing boards, administrators, and faculty at virtually every American college and university—public, private, large, small—are enormous. In short, athletics reform has become a whole new ball game with virtually every institution in America a player.

As a result, more people, groups, and associations are becoming actively involved in athletics reform. Examples include the Drake Group, Coalition on Intercollegiate Athletics, Association of Governing Boards, National Institute for Sports Reform, Knight Commission on Intercollegiate Athletics, and the College Athletes Coalition. The geneses and agendas of these groups will be outlined in the following chapter.

ABSENCE OF A CULTURE OF REFORM

Any effort to affect major institutional or cultural change is next to impossible if it occurs within a culture that can hardly imagine or even discuss change. Over one hundred years of a largely unchallenged existence, the athletic establishment has had little incentive to change. The result has been the development of an organizational culture that is ill-equipped to cope with or even entertain the thought of doing anything different from the way it has always been done.

Athletics is a very incestuous culture, perpetuated by generations of coaches and administrators who have been indoctrinated with a very narrow set of experiences and values. It is a culture that promotes loyalty to the team and coach, often to the exclusion of all else. From the moment youngsters step onto a playing field, coaches begin to drill into them the importance of unyielding dedication and commitment to the sport, team, and coach. Coaches set absolute standards for attitude and behavior, all centered upon molding a group of individuals into a team based on the principles of absolute obedience, discipline, and conformity. As a result, a form of group think envelops the team, with all athletes buying into the same set of attitudes, beliefs, and behaviors. Athletes are repeatedly told that only by subordinating individual behavior and goals to the greater good of the group will the team succeed. This attitude is exemplified by the common coaching adages, "There is no *I* in *team*" and "You are either for us or against us."

Such a controlled, authoritative environment hinders an individual's ability to think and act independently. There is a fine line between a healthy dose of discipline and an autocratic, militaristic dictatorship. Blindly obeying any and all commands is not necessarily a blueprint for success in life. A bit of healthy skepticism is important, as is the belief that you have the right to ask questions and challenge authority. Coaches, however, train athletes to respond to their demands without blinking an eye. In the heat of battle, quick and unquestioning response to commands can make the difference between winning and losing. While that may be true on the fields of play, expecting the same blind loyalty when the games are over is problematic.

These athletes then became coaches, who, if they wished to climb the career coaching ladder, had to continue to conform to the values and mores of the athletic culture. When those coaches retired from coaching, they were promoted to an administrative position in the athletics department. The result has been a very incestuous culture that is not very tolerant of alternative ideas and viewpoints.

I experienced resistance to change quite often while serving as Associate Commissioner for Compliance and Academic Affairs of the Southeastern Conference from 1989 to 1995. At the time, the NCAA Presidents Commission was fighting to establish and act upon its authority in the NCAA governance process; controversial initial eligibility standards were being implemented; and increasing emphasis was being placed on institutional control, compliance, academic integrity, and ethics. Further, athlete welfare was finally being recognized as an important issue; the Knight Commission on Intercollegiate Athletics was applying pressure for reform; and Dick Schultz, the new NCAA executive director, had challenged the membership to "build a new model" of intercollegiate athletics.

In short, reform had come to drive virtually every conversation, initiative, and decision in college athletics. Except in the SEC. In many ways, the SEC was the last bastion of the "good ole boys" of college athletics. It was no surprise that resistance to reform was so fierce in the SEC. One simply has to consider the role that SEC football plays in the culture of the Deep South. SEC football is not simply a sport but a way of life and a tremendous source of regional pride. For many years, in virtually every measure of societal health—poverty, illiteracy, infant mortality, education, and civil rights—the states in which SEC schools were located were among the worst in the country. Their college football teams, however, were among the best in the nation, one of the few bright spots for the region and a source of intense pride. When the SEC "Way of Life" was challenged and, by implication, the Southern "Way of Life," resistance was, understandably, fierce.

Given this context, the reform debate took on quite a different flavor in the SEC. While there were exceptions, the powers that be in the league resisted these reform efforts. It would be no stretch to describe the general attitude throughout the SEC to these national reform efforts as one of resistance and disdain. My job was to convince SEC coaches and administrators that Schultz was correct in calling for the development of a new model for intercollegiate athletics and that it was in their best interests to implement the necessary changes and programs to move toward that new model. Not surprisingly, I was often the target of the ire and defiance of coaches, athletics administrators, and even faculty athletics representatives and was repeatedly and heatedly accused of trying to "tear down" and "destroy" college athletics. On top of my reform message, the fact that I was a Yankee, PhD, former NCAA executive, and a "basketball guy," rather than a "football guy," did not particularly endear me to the "old line" SEC establishment types. That aside, to say that the culture of the SEC during this period of reform was accepting of reform ideas and initiatives would be a stretch.

Despite all signs on the national level to the contrary, strong and persistent strains of denial of the need for change permeated throughout the league. With stadiums full, money pouring in, athletes who rarely questioned the system, and fanatical fans fueling the enterprise, in the eyes of the SEC establishment, there was no reason to change. College athletics was doing just fine, and it was too important to the Southern "Way of Life" to change it.

But things did change. Athletic dorms were eliminated, eligibility standards rose, athletes achieved more rights, and presidents solidified control of the NCAA governance process. Despite the SEC's resistance, it was plain to see that the Presidents Commission was slowly making reform a staple of the NCAA agenda. Consequently, it became more acceptable to discuss and raise issues and questions regarding reform. One particularly important act in changing this cultural dynamic occurred in 1990 when NCAA Executive Director Schultz, in his "State of the Association Address," challenged the college athletics community to build a new model. There were many administrators, faculty, and coaches in the trenches talking about and trying to implement reform measures at the time. But when Schultz so directly and publicly acknowledged that the current system was broken and in need of reform, it opened the door for questions to be asked, principles to be challenged, and meaningful dialogue to occur. Schultz's public challenge dramatically shifted the tone and subject matter of the dialogue regarding reform. Defending the status quo, resisting reform, and marginalizing those who spoke of reform was no longer acceptable. Those who fought reform efforts were no longer looked upon as role models within the field but rather as closed-minded "dinosaurs" and "good ole boys," ill-equipped to provide the vision and leadership to guide college athletics into the rapidly changing higher education and cultural landscape of the future.

At the same time, the career path to positions of influence in athletics administration was changing. As college athletics grew as a business, the skills necessary to run an athletics department began to change. Presidents began hiring athletics directors with business backgrounds as opposed to simply placing former coaches in these positions. The advent of sports administration programs provided another avenue through which to become an athletics administrator. The result has been the slow emergence of a new generation of administrators who were not born and raised in a jock culture that had little regard for and appreciation and understanding of the appropriate role of athletics within the academy. This emerging and future generation of athletics administrators has grown up in an athletics culture where it is not only permissible but expected to question the status quo and to consider reform issues and strategies. To this emerging group of future and now current leaders, reform is no longer a dirty or prohibited word.

Finally, the culture of college athletics is changing because the college athletics community is becoming more diverse, particularly as it relates to women and minorities. The seeds planted in internship programs and diversity initiatives over the past fifteen years are beginning to bear fruit. Despite the fact that progress since the NCAA began tracking minorities and women in 1995–96 has been disappointingly slow (according to the NCAA website, the Minority Opportunities and Interests Committee reported in 2004 that from 1995–96 through 2001–02, the percentage of women in college athletics departments has risen from 35 percent to 40 percent and of minorities from 11 percent to 13 percent [http://www.ncaa.org]), the number and influence of blacks and women in college athletics departments is growing.

For example, in 1994, I hired as an SEC compliance intern an African-American man who had played football for the University of Georgia. His hiring was made possible by an NCAA-sponsored grant designed to enhance entry-level hiring of women and minorities. In 2004, Damon Evans was hired as athletics director of the University of Georgia, the first black athletics director in the history of the SEC. While progress remains painstakingly slow, women and minorities are diversifying the traditional "white males only" athletics establishment. The result is a college athletics community that is, and will continue to be, more diverse and more accepting of the possibilities of change.

Slowly, the culture of college athletics is changing as a new generation of administrators has made their way through the system. As a result, today's athletics culture is more open and accepting not only of concepts of diversity and change but also of the fact that athletics is not a stand-alone enterprise but rather a part of a larger academic community. This is far different from the athletics culture that existed during previous reform efforts. The seeds of reform that were advanced in the 1929 Carnegie Report, the "Sanity Code" of 1946, and the ACE proposals of 1952 were strewn on a barren cultural landscape. Today, the cultural landscape of athletics is much more fertile for those seeds of reform to take root.

TITLE IX

One of the most significant ways in which the broader reform context has changed relates to the enactment in 1972 of Title IX of the Education Amendments Act. Title IX prohibits discrimination on the basis of sex under any education program or activity receiving federal funding. Although it was adopted in 1972, its enforcement was largely ignored until the 1990s. Its impact, however, has been and will continue to be very dramatic. It has led to a substantial increase in participation opportunities for women in high school and college athletics. For example, "in 1972 only one girl in twenty-seven played a sport sponsored by her high school, and colleges spent a total of $100,000 on athletic scholarships for women. By 1996, one girl in three played a sport sponsored by her high school, and colleges spent a total of $180 million on athletic scholarships for women. The participation of women in college sports increased fourfold between 1970 and 1999, from 31,000 to 110,000" (Porto, 2003, pp. 14–15).

Title IX's impact goes far beyond sheer participation numbers or financial commitment as it relates to athletics reform. Specifically, the challenge of meeting the law and providing equal opportunity for women has forced institutions to reassess the role, purpose, and scope of their athletics departments, and will continue to do so. According to sports scholars Allen Sack and Ellen Staurowsky (1998), "Title IX and the struggle for gender equity have a greater potential for restoring the educational integrity of college sport than any reform passed by the NCAA in the past 100 years" (p. xiii).

This sentiment was echoed by Brian Porto in his book *A New Season: Using Title IX to Reform College Sports* (2003): "Title IX can help to bring fiscal sanity, academic integrity, and personal responsibility to college sports by encouraging colleges to replace the commercial model with the participation model. The trigger for this change is that most colleges can not afford to support women's sports as generously as they support men's sports, yet Title IX requires them to do so. In other words, the athletics director's dilemma is the reformer's golden opportunity" (p. 141).

Title IX will provide the impetus for institutions to begin to consider in earnest a fundamental shift in the type of athletics program they offer, from the current elitist, professional model to one based on the principle of broad-based participation. As will be argued later, it is this shift that must be at the core of any meaningful reform of athletics within our educational system.

ECONOMIC PRESSURES

As mentioned in chapter 1, despite the widely held belief that athletics programs generate enormous revenue for colleges and universities, more than 80 percent of the Division I programs actually *lose* money! But the fact that most athletics programs lose money is only half the story as it relates to the impact of the changing economic context for reform.

These figures must be considered against the larger backdrop of higher education finances and our nation's economy. As universities continue to spend significant resources on athletics, college tuition is rising dramatically. According to a 2002 study by the College Board, tuition and fees at public schools have increased by 38 percent over the past decade. For the 2002–03 academic year, the average tuition and fees charged by public four-year colleges and universities increased by 9.6 percent (p. 4). Further, public institutions are carrying greater debt. In 1999, the average debt for a public institution was $87 million. By 2002, it was over $140 million (Schemo, 2002, p. A-18). The result is that at a time when our country desperately needs more high school graduates to continue on to college, it is becoming increasingly difficult for middle- and lower-class students to afford to do so.

Meanwhile, according to the National Governor's Association, state economies are experiencing their worst fiscal crisis since World War II. This will dramatically affect state spending on higher education. According to a survey conducted by Illinois State University's Center for the Study of Education Policy, colleges are facing the most sweeping spending cuts in a decade. In spending plans states adopted for the 2002–03 fiscal year, aggregate appropriations for higher education only rose 1.2 percent, failing to keep pace with inflation which was 2 percent for the twelve months ending in October 2002. That figure is about a quarter of the 4.6 percent increase in 2001–02 and the smallest such rise since the 1992–93 fiscal year, which saw a 0.09 percent drop (Arone, 2002, p. A-28). In short, states are hurting economically and higher education will feel the pinch in a dramatic way.

Given these trends, it is becoming more difficult to justify sinking increasingly large amounts of money, resources, and energy into maintaining the current model of athletics programs that, while entertaining, have lost virtually all connection to the central mission of the institution.

LEGISLATIVE PRESSURE

Another important contextual factor that has changed significantly is the increased involvement of the United States Congress and state legislatures in athletics affairs. While the adoption of Title IX in 1983 has had a tremendous impact, other legislative initiatives have had an impact as well. In 1990, Congress enacted the Student Right-to-Know and Campus Security Act, which required colleges that receive federal funds to report their graduation rates to the Secretary of Education annually, including the graduation rates of their athletes, by sport, race, and gender.

In 1994, Congress passed the Equity in Athletics Disclosure Act, which requires colleges to report to the Secretary of Education the number of male and female undergraduates on campus, the number of participants on each male and female team, total operating expenses for male and female teams, scholarships and recruiting expenditures, among other Title IX-related factors.

There has also been an increase in legislation at the state level. For example, the Tennessee state legislature passed a bill that will prohibit the use of tax dollars to fund college athletics programs by 2006. Other notable bills would allow state schools in Nebraska, Texas, and Iowa to provide stipends to football players. In California, a bill which would bar in-state colleges and universities from abiding by NCAA rules on scholarships, health insurance, agent relationships, and enforcement actions was introduced in 2003. While it is unlikely that these bills will pass and ultimately impact the NCAA, the fact is that legislators at both the national and state levels are beginning to view the NCAA with a bit more skepticism and, thus, are less reluctant to exert outside legislative pressure to drive change.

Derek Bok (2003) articulates how this increased public skepticism can impact higher education:

> Universities have already grown more susceptible to public criticism because of their increased importance to society. When college and professional school become essential to coveted careers, students (and parents) are more inclined to feel resentful when they are denied admission or receive a failing grade. As universities grow richer, they begin to inspire envy more easily than affection. When campuses expand and acquire more land, they arouse greater hostility from the surrounding community. Amid these tensions, evidence of aggressive commercialism, and of the scandals and misadventures that often come in its wake, can easily provoke strong disapproval and distrust.
>
> As trust declines, the risk of government intervention increases. Newspaper stories about conflicts of interest of scientists performing experiments on human subjects or the money universities make through luxury boxes, television contracts, and advertising deals with clothing manufacturers create obvious opportunities for public officials to intervene. When Congress debates whether to act, universities that have openly indulged in entrepreneurial excess may find that the aura of public trust that once shielded them from hasty and unwise regulation is no longer available to protect them. (p. 116)

This skepticism was best summed up by Joe Biden, the Democratic senator from Delaware, during the Senate Judiciary Committee hearings in 2003 on how the Bowl Championship Series (BCS) crowns a college football champion. When concern was raised that a playoff would make college football seem like the pros, Biden remarked, "You already have an NFL model. Just go down the list of scandals every year, which are legion." After the University of Nebraska's chancellor, Harvey Perlman, cautioned that a playoff might hinder players' studies, Biden responded, "At your school, football is already a 12-month-a-year sport" (qtd. in Hiestand, 2003, p. 2-C).

While Congress chose not to become involved in the BCS controversy, Biden's comments provide a glimpse of the legal challenges facing the NCAA. As college athletics becomes more professionalized, the NCAA becomes more vulnerable to legal challenges. Sack and Staurowsky (1998) provide an excellent analysis of this possibility. They assert that the NCAA Division I-A programs have enjoyed a privileged legal status due to their association, under the NCAA umbrella, with nonscholarship Division III schools such as Amherst College and Williams College: "By giving the impression that big-time college sport is merely a variant of the amateur contests staged by nonscholarship-granting institutions, college sport has generally avoided income taxes, antitrust scrutiny, and other laws that apply to businesses" (p. 130).

Big-time college athletics has been marching steadily toward the professional model of sports, where the pursuit of corporate sponsors, gate receipts, television revenue, and bottom-line profit has come to overshadow the academic principles upon which it was supposed to be based. The question is when will judges and legislators reject the argument that college sports is an educationally centered, nonprofit operation concerned more about the personal growth and development of athletes than corporate sponsorships and television revenue? At what point will public and legal consensus begin to consider college athletics a business rather than an educational enterprise?

According to Tulane University sports-law expert Gary Roberts (1994), the increasingly professionalized nature of college sports places the NCAA, particularly Division I-A programs, in serious antitrust risk, subjects athletic revenue to unrelated business income taxes, and leads to players being viewed as employees with a right to unionize and to be covered by workers' compensation laws (pp. 4–5). If any of these were to occur, the cost of running a big-time college sports program would skyrocket, resulting in significant pressure to reform the current model.

As big-time athletics programs come to look and operate more like professional sports franchises, questions regarding whether the legislative and legal advantages granted nonprofit entities should continue to apply to the NCAA and individual athletics departments will intensify. In fact, the faculty-led Drake Group has undertaken an aggressive effort to spur Congress to examine the nonprofit status of the NCAA and college athletics departments. Will Congress ever rescind college athletics' nonprofit tax status? Is it possible that a judge will rule that college athletics has become so professionalized that the athletes should be considered professionals and eligible for workmen's compensation benefits? While there are no clear answers to these and related questions, these outcomes are significantly more possible today than they were twenty years ago. If college athletics continues to march down its current path of increasing professionalism and academic hypocrisy, the question will not be whether these outcomes might occur but when.

HIGHER EDUCATION'S AGE OF ASSESSMENT

While higher education represents many things to many people, its most central purpose is to educate our populace, develop new knowledge, and apply that knowledge and enhanced human potential to serve the needs of society. Given increasing costs, declining state revenues, and a more demanding public, the pressure on campuses, programs, and individuals to demonstrate how effectively they contribute to institutional mission and the public good has increased and, by all indications, will continue to do so. Thus, the central challenge for all institutions of higher learning is to demonstrate their utility. In short, American higher education is being held more accountable for its performance.

As would be expected, this standard of accountability impacts departments and individuals within the institution as everyone is being held more accountable for contributing to the mission of the institution in relevant and timely ways. In response, higher education has increased pressure on campuses, programs, and individuals to plan and implement models to assess how effectively educational goals and learning outcomes are being met. This increased emphasis on assessment to measure institutional effectiveness has come to influence virtually every aspect of higher education governance, practice, and decision making. As a result, the likelihood of significantly downsizing or restructuring a department or institutional operation that is not successfully meeting its purpose has never been greater. To think that athletics will not be held to the same standard of accountability is misguided.

PUBLIC PRESSURE FOR REFORM

According to a 2004 *Chronicle of Higher Education* survey, the public appears to be quite disenchanted with college athletics as 26 percent surveyed "strongly agreed" and another 50 percent "agreed" that colleges "place too much emphasis on athletics" (Suggs, 2004, A-12). Again, this is significant because of the leadership role higher education plays in our culture. The values that higher education sets provide an example for all to emulate regarding the role that athletics plays—from our grade schools and high schools, to our families and communities.

From a societal standpoint, we simply can no longer afford sport's violent, win-at-all-costs mentality eroding the ideals of a democratic and civil society. With our population becoming more obese, we can no longer accept the notion that athletic participation should be relegated to a minority of elite athletes. As we struggle to meet the rapidly changing educational, economic, and social demands of the twenty-first century, we can no longer continue to support an athletic culture that promotes anti-intellectualism, undermines educational values and institutions, and systematically creates "dumb jocks." And we simply can not afford the continued use of tax dollars to build stadiums for wealthy owners and millionaire players and to supplement the budgets of college athletics programs when our bridges, inner cities, and schools are crumbling.

This changing perception of the increasingly negative impact of elite athletics on our societal values and cultural institutions relates to Gladwell's second contributing principle to widespread cultural change, "The Stickiness Factor." Gladwell contends that a key to cultural change is the way a message is packaged and perceived. For years, calls for major athletics reform did not ring true to the public. Given the results of the above mentioned public-attitudes study and the ever-increasing media coverage of sports scandals, those calls seem to be resonating with the public to a greater degree today.

This increased sense of urgency was articulated by the Knight Commission in its 2001 report as follows: "If it proves impossible to create a system of intercollegiate athletics that can live honorably within the American college and university, then responsible citizens must join with academic and public leaders to insist that the nation's colleges and universities get out of the business of big-time sports" (Knight Foundation Commission on Intercollegiate Athletics, 2001a, p. 31). Never before has a group of college presidents and business leaders placed the issue of the elimination of big-time college athletics so squarely on the table. Never before has such a challenge been made not only to educational leaders but to the general public in such a bold and direct manner.

Gladwell (2000) identifies "The Power of Context" as the third factor that contributes to a "tipping point" for major cultural change. Specifically, the power of context suggests that epidemics or major cultural change "are sensitive to the conditions and circumstances of the times and places in which they occur" (p. 139). In this chapter, we have reviewed several ways in which the context or environment within which the current college athletics reform movement is occurring is far different from what existed during previous reform attempts. This change in context presents the possibility that serious reform measures can, in fact, take root and flourish. The idea that progressive, structural reform will never occur because the forces against it are too strong no longer applies. There are simply too many factors suggesting the time is ripe for significant reform to occur.

That said, the fact is that major social, cultural, or organizational change does not occur simply because the environmental context for change has become more favorable. Context or environment is simply the ground upon which seeds of change have the opportunity to take root. For the seeds of reform to take root and flourish requires the care and nurturing of all of the various groups with a stake in the health and prosperity of higher education. Systemic reform requires the coming together of people, groups, and institutions being committed and willing to remain involved with the issue. In short, a changed context is not enough. It must be accompanied by the critical mass necessary to drive progressive systemic change. In the next chapter, we will review in more detail the elements, events, people, and organizations that have come together over more than two decades to create that critical mass.

BUILDING CRITICAL MASS FOR CHANGE

All in all, it's just another brick in the wall.

—Pink Floyd

From the formation of the NCAA in 1906 through the release in 2001 of the Knight Commission's *A Call to Action: Reconnecting College Sports and Higher Education*, the commonly accepted notion regarding the history of reform is that these efforts have been periodic and short term, lasting a few years at best. The inability to stay the course has been cited as a major reason for the repeated failures to fundamentally reform college athletics. These failures are not surprising. Stopping the runaway freight train of big-time college athletics, an enterprise that has grown virtually unchecked for over one hundred years, requires more than an occasional show of resistance.

The idea that the higher education community has been unable to maintain a long-term, persistent reform effort, however, is incorrect. The fact is, the "current" reform effort represents not another reform *period* but rather the latest chapter in what can now be called a long-term reform *movement.* This movement began in 1982 when a group of college presidents, working through the ACE, proposed minimum academic standards for freshman eligibility. This action represented the laying of the first brick in what has become a slow and steady twenty-four-year process of building the foundation and critical mass of people, institutions, and organizations required to drive and support the sweeping change necessary to transform intercollegiate athletics. The purpose of this chapter is to chronicle the key initiatives and events that have contributed to building that foundation.

SETTING THE FOUNDATION

In 1983, the NCAA adopted Proposition 48 (then NCAA Bylaw 5-1-J, now NCAA Bylaw 14.3). This provision, which became effective in 1986, required an SAT score of 700 or ACT score of 15 and a 2.000 high school grade point average (GPA) in eleven "core" academic courses to be eligible for competition as a freshman. To say that Proposition 48 shook the world of intercollegiate athletics would be an understatement. Prior to 1973, incoming athletes were required to "predict" a minimum GPA of 1.6000 on a 4.000 scale. What made this standard laughable was that each institution was left to its own devices in "predicting" the likely GPA of the athlete. The standard was modified in 1973 to require high school athletes to have graduated with a 2.0 GPA in *all* courses, which could include as many "crib" courses as were needed to attain the standard.

Proposition 48 created a firestorm of debate regarding academic standards, culturally biased tests, athlete rights, and educational priorities. Regardless of where one came down on these issues, there was no denying the measure sent a strong message that a new day was dawning. Eventually, coaches and athletics directors grudgingly accepted the fact that athletes were no longer going to be given a free pass in the classroom. Proposition 48 was the first shot across the athletic establishment's bow in the battle of reform.

There were many more shots to be fired, the most significant of which was the establishment of the NCAA Presidents Commission in 1984. While it had always been understood that presidents were ultimately responsible for the conduct of athletics programs, from a practical and operational standpoint, the NCAA governance structure did not permit them to exert that influence. Further, presidents did not deem athletics to be important enough to spend much time managing it at the national level. For the most part, presidents left NCAA matters to their faculty athletics representatives (FAR). FARs, however, had little power and thus were hardly effective in their role as overseers of academic and institutional integrity. With access to skybox seats and the many perks of the athletics enterprise, they were widely viewed as being co-opted by the system. It was the athletics directors, conference commissioners, and "power" coaches who ran the show. With the likes of the University of Alabama's "Bear" Bryant, the University of Arkansas's Frank Broyles, the University of Texas's Darryl Royal, and Ohio State University's Woody Hayes, all "living legends," presidents and FARs hardly had a chance to wield their influence in athletics matters. Consequently, NCAA rules, policies, and processes were shaped by athletic, rather than academic and institutional, priorities and interests.

But as athletics' impact on campus grew, presidents realized they had to become more vigilant. Their answer was to form the Presidents Commission, which consisted of 44 members (twenty-two from Division I, eleven from Division II, and eleven from Division III). Over the next few years, the Commission institutionalized a series of measures to help presidents set and control the NCAA agenda. Most important was a statute allowing the Commission to place proposed rule changes directly on the convention agenda. Rather than having to work through a committee consisting primarily of athletics directors, FARs, and coaches, presidents gained direct access to the NCAA legislative process and governance structure. The Commission also implemented a procedural rule giving them the authority to require a roll-call vote on any proposed rule change. This provided a mechanism to ensure that an institution's vote reflected its president's position on an issue. To appreciate the significance of this measure requires an understanding of the NCAA convention and legislative process at the time.

Once a year, the NCAA membership gathered under one roof. With three thousand or more delegates in the same room debating over 150 proposed rule changes, many of them of very little real consequence, it was understandable that presidents did not want to devote three days to this event. This left the responsibility for registering an institution's vote to the athletics director or FAR, which was done by raising a color-coded paddle. Except in the case of a narrow vote, the NCAA staff was responsible for eye-balling the result. In a room full of three thousand people with one thousand paddles voting on over 150 proposals with no written record of individual votes, it was not sur-prising that a position determined by the president back on campus was not always reflected in the actual vote by the athletics director on the convention floor. The ability to demand a roll-call vote on specific legislation was signifi-cant because it assured presidents that *their* position on a proposal would be registered.

Presidents also revised the convention process to enable them to establish the order of legislative proposals. This minimized the amount of time presidents would have to spend at the convention by allowing those items of particu-lar interest to them to be considered during one day. Conse-quently, presidential attendance at the convention began to increase. The NCAA archivist reports that in 1980 only 34 presidents attended the convention. In 1985, 96 attended, and that number steadily rose to 169 in 1990, to 213 in 1992, to 254 in 1994, to a peak of 311 in 1997 (Summers, 2004). This was not only a very practical improvement but it helped presidents serve notice that they were going to be more actively involved in the governance process.

The significance of the establishment of the Presidents Commission and these initial initiatives can not be over-stated. While the NCAA bylaws were clear that the author-ity over athletics rested with presidents, the establishment of the Presidents Commission and these early procedural changes provided the vehicle for them to begin to exert influence more efficiently and effectively.

SERVING NOTICE

Once the presidents established the foundation for their engagement with athletics governance, it was time to serve notice that they were serious about reform. To that end, they called for a Special Convention on integrity in the summer of 1985. If there were any doubts regarding how serious presidents were about reform, they would soon be erased with the adoption of several measures, all of which were designed to exert more institutional control over athletics departments. It was during this special convention that presidents made an emphatic statement that athletics departments were going to be held accountable for their actions through a major increase in emphasis on compliance and institutional control as well as a dramatic strengthening of the penalty structure for rules violations.

The most striking of these measures was the addition of the "repeat violator" provision to the existing "death penalty." Under the repeat violator provision, a program could be assessed the "death penalty" if any other program in the athletics department had committed a major violation within the previous five years. The "death penalty" allowed the NCAA Committee on Infractions to shut down a program that committed repeated major violations on a departmentwide, as opposed to an individual-sport, basis. This change raised the stakes in the area of compliance considerably. Further, to send a message that coaches were going to be held accountable for knowing and abiding by the rules, a provision stipulating that coaches who committed major infractions could be banned from coaching at an NCAA institution for up to five years was also adopted.

The Presidents Commission then turned its attention to institutional control and oversight, where they adopted four measures. First was a provision to require athletics departments to undergo a yearly financial audit conducted by an outside, independent agency. This was the first attempt to force athletics departments to increase transparency in the area of finances. To hold institutions more accountable for the type of educational experience available to their athletes, a provision requiring them to report graduation rates by gender, sport, and race was adopted. Despite concern that the measurement was flawed (for example, an athlete who left school early to play professionally would be counted against an institution's rate), the Commission maintained that, warts and all, there would be some measure of academic accountability. Third, to encourage institutions to assess and evaluate athletics department processes, procedures, policies, and results, the Commission pushed through a provision to require Division I institutions to conduct a self-study of their athletics departments. These measures sent the message that the days of athletics departments being able to operate without any institutional oversight were coming to a close.

Finally, the Commission adopted a resolution to establish more effective institutional control over athletics departments. At the time, the NCAA's idea of institutional control and compliance was to distribute rule books and hope that coaches and administrators would read, understand, and abide by those rules. While nobody knew exactly what would constitute a comprehensive compliance program, presidents knew that institutions had to exert more control over athletics department operations and that athletics departments had to be held more accountable for how they operated. The Commission set the tone, established the vision, and mandated that conferences and schools develop and implement oversight programs to enable institutions to control their athletics departments more effectively. While it was clear that something significant had occurred at the summer 1985 Special Convention, it was much less clear what it all meant and where it would lead. In little more than two years, presidents had shattered the athletic establishment's viselike grip on the NCAA governance and legislative process and laid down some significant markers in the areas of integrity, institutional control, and academic accountability. While these measures caught the attention of some old-guard coaches and athletics administrators, the prevailing notion among this group was that, like previous reform efforts, this one would be short-lived. Presidents, they said, would enact a series of reform measures, pat themselves on the backs, and then lose interest in the issue just as they had always done. This time, however, they would be proven wrong.

BUILDING THE FRAMEWORK FOR INSTITUTIONAL CONTROL

Although presidents knew that institutional control had to be a cornerstone of reform, they had little idea as to what form this control might take. One thing, however, was clear. If coaches and administrators were to be held accountable for knowing and abiding by NCAA rules, it was necessary to develop the resources to educate them about those rules. To address this challenge, the Commission turned to the NCAA staff.

One of the most misunderstood organizations in sports is the NCAA and its staff. Consisting of over one thousand colleges, universities, and conferences, the NCAA is a membership organization. Representatives from these schools and conferences retain all authority regarding NCAA rules and policies. The NCAA office staff has absolutely no authority in this area but rather exists to serve the will of the membership. Representatives of the schools adopt rules and the staff helps implement and administer them. This is why, contrary to wide public perception, the NCAA executive director has no authority to make or pass rules. Developing and helping member institutions implement compliance and institutional-control measures during this period of reform, however, was clearly a staff responsibility.

Institutional control is based upon compliance with rules. That is where the staff began. At the time, the most often cited criticism of the NCAA national office staff was inconsistency and a lack of responsiveness in rule interpretations. This was due largely to the fact that questions regarding rules were directed to the Enforcement staff. Unfortunately, Enforcement representatives viewed investigating rules violations as their primary responsibility. They had neither the time nor inclination to answer questions from administrators and coaches regarding how rules were to be interpreted. Rather than talking about the rules, their priority was to be on the road investigating those who were breaking them. It was no wonder that many of the hundreds of rules-related calls the NCAA received daily were not returned or that interpretations regarding eligibility or playing and practice seasons were inconsistent. As a result, the prevailing attitude among coaches and administrators was that if the NCAA leadership was not committed enough to provide a service where schools could receive consistent, timely, and thoroughly researched answers to questions, why should they care about learning and abiding by those rules?

This attitude, coupled with the fact that the NCAA Manual was poorly organized and written contributed to the membership's lack of confidence and trust in the legislative process and NCAA staff. To address this concern, the NCAA created a new department in 1986. Legislative Services was charged with the responsibility of educating coaches and administrators about the rules and interpreting those rules when questions arose regarding their application. While not as visible or controversial as initial eligibility standards, the creation of Legislative Services sent an important message nonetheless. Presidents were appropriating money and resources to back up their challenge to coaches and administrators to know and abide by the rules. The creation of Legislative Services marked the beginning of a push to build an administrative structure capable of supporting the Commission's goal of establishing compliance and institutional control as fundamental operating principles.

Slowly, Legislative Services began to rebuild trust with the membership by becoming more responsive, efficient, and consistent in their education and interpretation efforts. Further, they reorganized and simplified the NCAA Manual, making it more user-friendly. It soon became apparent, however, that teaching about rules and providing interpretations was simply the starting point in helping institutions establish effective institutional control. Ensuring effective institutional control would also require the development of systems to certify and monitor eligibility, financial aid, and recruiting processes. In other words, knowing every rule relating to eligibility would be of no use if the institutional process for certifying that eligibility was dysfunctional.

With this in mind, the Compliance Department was established in 1989 to help schools develop systems of checks and balances to ensure more effective oversight of athletics department operations. The Presidents Commission's mandate regarding institutional control was gathering momentum and filtering down to the conference and institutional levels. Slowly, a compliance network was being established, which continues to evolve and improve to this day. The evolution of the NCAA national office in this regard has played and will continue to play a significant role in the building of the critical mass for reform. Without the development of such a resource and support function, institutions would not have been able to develop and refine their compliance and institutional control efforts.

THE REFORM BEAT GOES ON

As the national office was restructuring and expanding to meet the membership's growing compliance and institutional control needs, presidents continued to march forward on the academic standards, rules enforcement, and athlete welfare fronts. Proposition 48, the initial eligibility requirements that were adopted in 1983, took affect in 1986. In an effort to strengthen those standards, Proposition 42 was passed in 1989. This revision to the initial eligibility standards was extremely controversial as it prohibited freshmen from receiving institutional financial aid if they did not meet initial eligibility standards. The controversy centered upon the claim that the NCAA had no right to prohibit an athlete from receiving institutional aid not related to athletics. This was a case of the NCAA overstepping its bounds and the rule was rescinded the following year. Nevertheless, the furor kept the issue of academic reform in the national spotlight, particularly as it was being played out against the backdrop of the impending 1991 deadline for the reporting of graduation rates. This ensured that academic reform would continue to remain front and center on the NCAA agenda.

In the area of rules enforcement, the Committee on Infractions assessed the "death penalty" on Southern Methodist University's football program in 1987. The infraction was a case not of a wayward booster paying a player but rather of an organized system of payments administered within the athletics department. The corruption was calculated, institutionalized, and widespread. Knowledge of the payment plan went as high as the board of trustees. The program was out of control and, as a result, was shut down for two seasons. Southern Methodist University's receiving the "death penalty" was a wake-up call for many programs. That is not to say that the cheating stopped, but the idea of institutionalized payment and cheating schemes began to change.

Interest in athlete welfare also intensified in 1988 with the release of the most comprehensive study of athlete attitudes and experiences in the history of the organization. The picture that emerged from this study, which received wide media attention, was one of athletes being underprepared and outperformed academically, overworked athletically, isolated in an athletic "womb," with little money to enjoy anything close to a "normal" life as a college student.

It was ironic that an organization that professed to be "about the student-athlete" was apparently nothing of the sort. It was not necessarily the specific findings that were so startling. Rather, it was the fact that what many had known about the college athletics experience—that athletes were on campus not to get an education but to play ball—was laid out clearly, supported by quantifiable, scientific data. The myth of the "student-athlete," so vigorously promoted by coaches and athletics administrators, was shattered.

In an effort to address the issues laid bare by the study, a Student-Athlete Advisory Committee (SAAC) was established in 1989. The SAAC represented the NCAA's first attempt to create an ongoing vehicle through which to obtain feedback from athletes. This committee was influential in the adoption in 1991 of several "student-athlete welfare" proposals. Three were particularly noteworthy; a rule that limited an athlete to participation in no more than twenty hours of athletically related activities per week, a rule that eliminated athletic dormitories, and a shortening of playing and practice seasons.

The presidents also continued to develop and support their vision of compliance and institutional control. In a move that had far-reaching impact, the NCAA established a $3.5 million fund for Division I conferences to improve compliance programs, basketball officiating, drug-education programs, and enhancement of opportunities for ethnic minorities and women. The impact of this program on compliance was enormous. Not only was the Presidents Commission talking about the importance of compliance, but it was backing up that talk with significant financial support. Much of this money was used by conferences to enhance their compliance staffs and services.

NEW VOICES ON THE SCENE

While the Presidents Commission had established itself as the driving force for reform, the late 1980s saw the entrance of two new and very influential players onto the reform scene. In 1987, Dick Schultz replaced Walter Byers as executive director of the NCAA. Byers had been the only executive director the NCAA had ever known, having held the position since 1951. Under Byers, the NCAA had come to be viewed as secretive and inflexible. Schultz arrived from his post as athletics director of the University of Virginia and made it clear that his style of leadership would be different.

Schultz articulated three primary goals for his early tenure. First, he worked to "open up" the NCAA by being more accessible to the membership and media. During his first year, he spent close to three hundred days on the road, meeting athletics directors, members of the media, presidents, and otherwise being highly visible, and, in the process, educating the public regarding the role and purpose of the NCAA. Second, he pledged to make the NCAA more "user-friendly" by improving services. Finally, Schultz vowed to make the NCAA more "flexible." Regardless of how outrageous or nonsensical a rule, it was extremely rare

when the NCAA allowed any flexibility in its interpretation.
Schultz set out to change the culture of the organization
to allow a more commonsense and flexible approach to
rule interpretations. Clearly, a new day was dawning at the
NCAA national office.

Just as significant was the announcement in 1989 of the
formation of the Knight Commission on Intercollegiate
Athletics. This commission was funded by the John S. and
James L. Knight Foundation and was charged with propos-
ing a reform agenda for college athletics. The trustees of
the Knight Foundation believed that the abuses in college
athletics had reached a point where they were threatening
the integrity of higher education. The Knight Commission,
co-chaired by William Friday and Theodore Hesburgh,
presidents emeritus of the University of North Carolina and
University of Notre Dame, respectively, consisted not only
of college presidents but also prominent business leaders.

This was a group of very influential, high-powered leaders backed by a highly respected foundation taking on a
visible and emotionally charged issue at an important juncture in the evolution of the enterprise. Intent on keeping
political and public pressure on the NCAA to remain dili-
gent in its reform effort, the Knight Commission held a
series of hearings and press conferences while developing
its reform agenda, which was to be released in 1991.

On the heels of the formation of the Knight Commission,
Schultz delivered what may be the most important speech
regarding athletics in the history of higher education. During
his "State of the Association Address" at the 1990 NCAA
Convention, he described the existing system as being
broken and challenged the college athletics community

to embrace reform by adopting a new model of college athletics. The new model would be based upon trust and integrity, which would require an institutional commitment to establishing a compliance program, emphasize academics and academic integrity, reduce off-campus recruiting, lessen pressure on coaches to win, and increase emphasis on athlete welfare.

The impact of Schultz's address was enormous. When the NCAA executive director states publicly that the system is in need of a massive overhaul, the level and frequency of dialogue regarding athletics reform is elevated significantly. This contributed to changing the culture of college athletics in a way that allowed increasingly open, frank, and critical dialogue regarding the current system. Finally, the opportunity to speak openly about reform had arrived.

These two voices continued to resonate with the release in 1991 of the Knight Commission's long awaited report, titled *Keeping Faith with the Student-Athlete: A New Model for Intercollegiate Athletics*. To much fanfare, the report outlined a "one plus three" model of athletics reform centered on the "one"—presidential control—directed toward the "three"—academic integrity, financial integrity, and independent certification. While some elements of this "new" model were not necessarily new, the impact of the Knight Commission and its report were enormous. For example, the NCAA Presidents Commission had been operating on the principle of presidential control since its inception. But the fact that the Knight Commission placed this principle at the core of its model had a significant impact in cementing the concept into the culture of college athletics. Among other things, the report called for stronger eligibility standards as well as a reduction in athletics expenditures and the influence of outside booster groups.

Further, the report called for the development of an athletics department certification program. Such a program would independently authenticate, by an outside body, the integrity of each institution's athletics program. The commission's report stated that "the academic and financial integrity of college athletics is in such low repute that authentication by an outside agency is essential." The program's purpose would be to regularly examine athletics departments "to ensure the major systems are functioning properly and that problems are treated before they threaten the health of the entire program. Such checkups should cover the entire range of academic and financial issues in intercollegiate athletics" (Knight Foundation Commission on Intercollegiate Athletics, 1991, p. 21). The NCAA had been in the process of pilot testing such a program and the Knight Commission's recommendation all but ensured that that program would eventually be adopted and implemented.

The Knight Commission was serving its purpose as an outside watchdog, keeping pressure on the NCAA to stay the reform course. It was also noteworthy that the Knight Commission was committed to remaining intact and to monitoring the progress the NCAA made on its recommendations. To that end, the Knight Commission released follow-up reports in 1992 and 1993. The first, titled "A Solid Start: A Report on Reform of Intercollegiate Athletics," and the second, titled "A New Beginning for a New Century: Intercollegiate Athletics in the United States," registered its general satisfaction with the progress being made on reform. Upon the release of the second follow-up report, the commission disbanded, only to be reconvened, not once, but twice.

Some cite the fact that the Knight Commission was reconstituted as evidence that it was not successful. On the contrary, the larger purpose of prodding the NCAA to establish the structure necessary to carry out future change had been accomplished and the benefits of the Knight Commission's efforts continue to be felt to this day. Meaningful, long-term change can not be accomplished without a structure to facilitate and support reform. Not only was the Knight Commission instrumental in assisting presidents in establishing such a structure, but its very visible efforts increased the public's awareness of the importance of reform and kept pressure on the NCAA to stay the reform course. In short, the Knight Commission, along with Schultz, were very important and influential players in the reform game.

CHANGING THE CULTURE AND BUILDING A COMPLIANCE COMMUNITY

Conventional wisdom would have predicted that after a decade of active engagement in reform, presidents and the NCAA membership would have tired of the issue. Rather than losing interest and focus, presidents continued to hammer away, solidifying their gains, not only academically but, more significantly, in the areas of institutional control, increased transparency in athletics operations, and reform of the win-at-all-costs athletics culture.

Academic standards continued to be refined and strengthened. Beginning in 1991, the Knight Commission adopted a
series of measures that strengthened satisfactory progress
standards. These measures, adopted over a period of several
years, gradually raised the academic requirements for athletes to remain eligible from year to year, requiring yearly
progress toward a degree as well as a minimum GPA in the
athlete's major. The first set of graduation rates was also
released in 1991. As a result, the idea that wins, losses, and
revenue were not the only ways to judge the "success" of an
athletics department began to take hold. And in 1992, Division I adopted NCAA Proposal 16, to take effect in 1995,
which strengthened freshman eligibility standards by raising the number of core courses from eleven to thirteen and
the required GPA for those courses from 2.00 to 2.50.

Presidents also tried to address the win-at-all-costs culture by revising the formula for distributing revenue generated from the television-rights fees from the NCAA men's
basketball tournament. Up to that point, schools received
shares based upon how far they advanced in the tournament. For each game won, the school would earn another
share of revenue, which, at the time, was in the neighbor-
hood of $250,000 per share.

This formula was revised to include other factors in
determining institutional revenues. The basketball performance component, while not eliminated, was stretched
over a six year period, with only one third of the money
being distributed according to this standard. Another third
was distributed based upon the number of athletics scholarships a school offered, with the final third based upon the
number of sports sponsored. The idea behind this formula

was to eliminate the $250,000 "free throw" by distributing money based upon an athletics department's commitment to providing participation opportunities. While not perfect, the formula did, at least symbolically, reduce the pressure to win in order to generate money.

In the area of institutional control and transparency, an athletics certification program was adopted in 1993. Introduced in 1989 and pilot tested from 1991 to 1993, athletics certification was a vital component of the reform agenda. Although regional higher education agencies evaluated and certified colleges and universities, generally, those reviews were limited to academic programs. The certification program's purpose was to review Division I programs in four areas: governance and rules compliance, fiscal integrity, academic integrity, and commitment to equity, which included gender equity, racial equity, and athlete welfare. Most importantly, the process would open up the affairs of the athletics department to the university community by including various institutional constituencies in the information-gathering and evaluation processes. The first set of certification reviews began in 1995.

The development and implementation of a national certification program was significant for another reason. It provided evidence that expectations regarding compliance and institutional control were increasing and that a compliance community was emerging to help meet those expectations. By 1994, all of the Division I conferences had associate or assistant commissioners for compliance. Whereas a decade prior the position of full-time institutional compliance coordinator did not exist, by 1994 most Division I athletics programs had one. The NCAA staff worked to educate and develop the conference compliance personnel, who did the same for their institutional compliance representatives. As a result, rules-education programs for coaches and administrators were being implemented, and increased attention was being given to developing and implementing more effective systems of checks and balances to monitor athletics department processes. Clearly, compliance was no longer a dirty word but had become a part of the culture of college athletics.

This is not to say that college athletics was, or is ever going to be, scandal free. As television exposure, athletics budgets, and the pressure to win grows, the pressure to cheat grows along with it. This is the constant tension that exists in the world of college athletics. What was changing, however, was that the pressure to win and the attitudes and practices that resulted from that pressure were no longer going unchecked. For the first time, coaches had to account for their recruiting visits, phone calls, and expense reports. Athletics department procedures were being scrutinized to ensure more accountability. Institutional processes for the awarding of financial aid and certifying eligibility were being reviewed and codified. Institutions were gaining more control over their athletics departments.

NEW GOVERNANCE MODEL, SAME PRESIDENTIAL AUTHORITY

In 1996, the NCAA voted to restructure its governance system. Up to that point, NCAA governance was based upon the principle of "one institution, one vote." This meant that on legislative matters that affected the entire association, Franklin and Marshall College, a nonscholarship Division III institution with a small athletics budget, had the same amount of power as the University of Tennessee, which awarded several hundred scholarships and has an enormous athletics budget.

The restructuring effort was driven by two factors. The first was that Division I-A programs, those one hundred or so schools playing big-time football, had grown so large that they had very little in common with not only Division III, small-college, nonscholarship programs but even Division I-AA and I-AAA programs. Yet, despite this vast difference, all had only one vote. Consequently, Division I-A athletics directors felt they had little control over legislation impacting their programs. This was particularly true on proposals requiring an increase in expenses. Such proposals were often voted down, despite the fact that, in many cases, they were viewed as being important and relatively minor expenses for a Division I-A program. This was a source of tremendous frustration for Division I-A athletics directors and conference commissioners. Compounding that frustration was the fact that Division I-A programs were generating most of the NCAA's revenue.

With Division I-A frustration over the one-institution-one-vote model at a fever pitch, coupled with a general desire to improve the efficiency of the legislative process, the NCAA considered an alternative approach. Division I-A conference commissioners proposed scrapping the one-institution-one-vote model in favor of a representative form of governance where conferences designated representatives to sit on various cabinets and committees.

The ultimate authority for rule and policy changes, however, would continue to reside with presidents. This was achieved through the establishment of a board of directors consisting entirely of presidents with ultimate authority over all NCAA matters.

While it can be argued that the major restructuring of the governance process was not necessarily a positive initiative for reform of the culture and conduct of athletics programs, it was, nonetheless, a significant development in the evolution of the NCAA. It was positive in that it continued to recognize the primacy of presidential authority. On another level, however, the restructuring may have had some unintended consequences from the standpoint of creating a system conducive to minimizing or eliminating the professional model of intercollegiate athletics. Under the new system, Division I-A institutions, the very schools that have the most invested in the existing professional model, hold virtually all of the governance cards. This change presents a challenge to those who want to scale back the professional model. Hopefully, presidents will continue to distinguish the benefits of reform from an Association-wide standpoint from the specific interests of the institutions they represent.

ADDITIONAL VOICES TO THE CHOIR

With the notable exception of the Knight Commission, reform had been driven largely by forces within the NCAA "family." By 1999, however, groups and individuals external to the traditional NCAA structure were beginning to become engaged in the effort. The Drake Group, consisting of faculty members from across the country, formed in 1999 as a mere blip on the reform radar screen. Since then, it has doggedly stayed in the reform game, gradually building up a more visible profile. The group's mission is to restore academic integrity to intercollegiate athletics and thus fulfill faculty's obligation to protect the welfare of all students. The centerpiece of their agenda calls for public disclosure of the academic major, academic advisor, courses listed by academic major, GPA, and instructor for all students. Their belief is that without increased academic transparency, the true depths to which institutions are sinking to keep athletes eligible will never be revealed. More recently, they have called on Congress to reconsider athletics departments' status as nonprofit educational entities.

During this period, a series of books regarding athletics reform were being published, thus raising the level of public awareness and dialogue relating to reform. Books such as *College Athletes for Hire: The Evolution and Legacy of the NCAA's Amateur Myth* (1998), co-authored by Allen Sack, a defensive end on the University of Notre Dame's 1966 national championship football team, and Ellen Staurowsky; *Unpaid Professionals: Commercialism and Conflict in Big-Time College Sports* (1999) by Andrew Zimbalist; *Beer and Circus: How Big-Time College Sports Is Crippling Undergraduate Education* (2000), by Murray Sperber; *Intercollegiate Athletics and the American University: A University President's Perspective* (2000), by former president of the University of Michigan James Duderstadt; and *The Game of Life: College Sports and Educational Values* (2001), by James Shulman and William Bowen, former president of Princeton University, kept the reform fires burning brightly and contributed to a growing critical mass of people calling for reform.

The push for reform from groups outside the formal NCAA structure continued in dramatic fashion in 2000. Amid increasing concern regarding the growing financial "arms race" as well as the increasingly commercial nature of college athletics, the Knight Commission reconvened. The commission's cochairs, William Friday and Theodore Hesburgh, acknowledged that the NCAA had made considerable progress toward achieving the goals the first commission had set out. Yet, there was a feeling that, despite that progress, problems in big-time college sports had become more severe.

The release in 2001 of the Knight Commission report *A Call to Action: Reconnecting College Sports and Higher Education* was significant in two ways. First, it contained the pointed admission that "the cultural sea change is now complete. Big-time college football and basketball have been thoroughly professionalized and commercialized" (Knight Foundation Commission on Intercollegiate Athletics, 2001a, p. 23). Second, it recognized that athletics reform was no longer simply about institutional integrity and higher education but also its negative influence on the American culture of sport, all the way down to the youth-league level. In other words, the Knight Commission highlighted the fact that college athletics reform was now a cultural issue of significant importance.

Yet, the Knight Commission believed that "the academic enterprise can still redeem itself and its athletics adjunct. It is still possible that all college sports can still be reintegrated into the moral and institutional culture of the university"

(Knight Foundation Commission on Intercollegiate Athletics, 2001a, p. 23). To do so, however, would not require more rules but rather "a concerted grassroots effort by the broader academic community—in concert with trustees, administrators, and faculty—to restore the balance of athletics and academics on campus" (p. 24). While standing firm on its belief that presidents were the key to athletics reform, this report was significant because it challenged everyone with a stake in higher education—faculty, boards of trustees, various higher education associations, athletics directors, and coaches—to become more engaged in the reform effort.

Meanwhile, other groups were hopping on the reform train. Led by a group of former athletes, the Collegiate Athletes Coalition (CAC) organized in 2000 with the goal of improving the conditions and lives of student-athletes. Its emphasis has been on financial issues, particularly on raising the amount of an athletic scholarship to cover the full cost of attendance and to assuring that health coverage for athletes extends to out-of-season training. The CAC receives most of its funding from the United Steelworkers Union, in what some believe is an attempt to unionize college athletes. According to their director, Ramogi Huma, the CAC is transitioning from a group that has attempted to work through the NCAA to achieve change to one that will increasingly work through state legislatures and the legal system to pressure the NCAA for change.

In 2002, another "outside" group dedicated to athletics reform came onto the scene. The Coalition on Intercollegiate Athletics (COIA) was originally formed as an e-mail network of faculty leaders from over fifty Division

I-A schools in Bowl Championship Series conferences. In the fall of 2003, COIA became a coalition of faculty senates welcoming membership from all Division I-A schools. Its purpose was to position itself as a faculty voice in the national debate over the future of college athletics. COIA is committed to operating within the system, as evidenced by its working relationship with the American Association of University Professors (AAUP), Association of Governing Boards (AGB), and NCAA. The group has prepared a "Framework for Reform," which outlines a five-point reform agenda: (1) academic integrity, (2) athlete welfare, (3) governance of athletics at the school and conference level, (4) finances, and (5) commercialization.

In response to the Knight Commission's call for governing boards "to do more to help resolve the persistent problems addressed in its 2001 report" (Knight Foundation Commission on Intercollegiate Athletics, 2001a, p. 24), the AGB began to step up to the issue of reform. To that end, AGB's board of directors developed and released in 2004 a statement exhorting trustees to become more responsibly engaged in the oversight and governance of athletics programs on their campuses. The statement is designed for boards to use as a basis for discussion and to serve as a primer for trustees, presidents, and institutional leaders by articulating key questions that boards and trustees should consider, along with checklists of good policies and practices. This represents AGB's most proactive and extensive effort in this area.

The most recent addition to the reform lineup is the National Institute for Sports Reform (NISR). Formed in 2003, NISR is a coalition of concerned educators, members

of the media, and various sports reformers devoted to studying, advocating, and implementing needed sports reforms
at the preprofessional levels. By working proactively to
educate the public about sports reform issues, the organization's goal is to provide solutions for the many problems
that currently envelope athletes at the youth, amateur, scholastic, and collegiate levels of sports. While its impact has
yet to be felt on a national basis, the creation of this institute
is significant, as it provides another example of concerned
individuals from "outside" the traditional NCAA structure coming together to contribute to the broader effort to
reform athletics in America.

A PRESIDENTIAL FIRST AND MORE
ACADEMIC REFORM

Much as Dick Schultz was welcomed as a breath of fresh air
to reformers, so too was Indiana University President Myles
Brand when he was hired as NCAA president (the position
formerly referred to as executive director) in 2003. Brand,
who achieved great notoriety for firing legendary Indiana
basketball coach Bobby Knight, is the first former president to head the organization. Brand's hiring provides a
wonderful symmetry to presidential involvement and leadership in the reform of college athletics. Twenty-one years
after a group of presidents proposed raising initial eligibility standards, a member of their own ranks was presiding
as the NCAA president. It is fair to say that presidents have
far exceeded expectations regarding their interest in and
commitment to reforming athletics. Their job, however, is

not complete, and, in many ways, the challenges of the next twenty-one years may be more difficult.

As would be expected, Brand has continued to push for academic reform. If there has been one issue that presidents have consistently and persistently focused on since 1982, it has been academic standards and performance. That interest continues, as evidenced by the adoption of a significant set of reforms designed to fundamentally alter the existing paradigm relating to academic accountability. Amid much fanfare, in 2005, the NCAA adopted another academic reform package designed to penalize a team with the loss of scholarships and eligibility for postseason play if its athletes continue to perform at substandard academic levels.

The significance of this measure is that, for the first time, someone other than the athlete will suffer a direct penalty. Using an index formula based primarily on retention rates, every NCAA team will receive a score. If that score falls below a threshold point, the program will be penalized. It is hoped that this attempt to tie penalties directly to a program will force coaches to recruit athletes who are better prepared academically and exert more effort in mentoring and retaining them. While the effect of this change has yet to be determined, it illustrates that presidents will remain engaged with reform. As proof of their resolve, in 2005 they formed a task force to explore the alignment of athletics with the mission, values, and goals of higher education. Clearly, presidents are determined to keep the reform drums beating.

The purpose of this review of the highlights of the ongoing athletics reform movement is to demonstrate that the higher education community, led by presidents, has been actively, persistently, and effectively engaged with the issue of athletics reform for almost a quarter of a century. As a result, there now exists in the higher education community a culture of athletics reform where none had existed before. Just as important is the legislative and governance structure that has been established to enable systemic change to occur. Presidents have become very adept at pushing through legislation and policy changes. Meanwhile, a growing critical mass of people, organizations, and institutions have been coalescing around the idea that fundamental reform of the professional model of college athletics is not an option but a necessity. As Hodding Carter III, president of the Knight Foundation, stated after the Knight Commission on Intercollegiate Athletics November 23, 2003, press conference, "What we heard (from Commission members) was a general sense that we have to push the envelope hard. Incremental change is not going to do it" (Suggs, 2003).

This review highlighted the most influential reform measures. (A more complete, chronological listing of reform measures and initiatives is provided at the end of the volume.) When you add up all of the factors, forces, organizations, and changes that have occurred over the last twenty-four years, it becomes clear that a critical mass of contributing players and institutions is in place to support reform measures that have heretofore been considered unthinkable. For the first time in the history of American higher education, there is a culture and counterforce sizable enough to effectively stop the runaway freight train of professionalized college athletics and to support the progressive, systemic reform measures outlined in the following chapter.

REBUILD IT AND THEY WILL CONTINUE TO COME

Change is not made without inconvenience,
even from worse to better.

—Richard Hooker

Higher education leaders have been trying to reform athletics for decades. Despite these efforts, Division I athletics continues to undermine the academic integrity and educational missions of our colleges and universities in very significant ways. At issue is not the value of elite athletics in our culture but whether our educational institutions should be saddled with the responsibility of developing elite athletes and sponsoring professional teams. Like trying to fit a round peg into a square hole, the professional sports model simply does not fit within the educational community. Rather than continuing to pound that peg, it is time to admit that sponsorship of elite, professional athletics should be left to the professional leagues. In short, it is time for colleges and universities to eliminate their departments of professional athletics.

The following bears mentioning again. While one of American higher education's strengths is its tremendous diversity of services, programs, opportunities, and missions, in the case of athletics, higher education may not be able to have it all. Division I athletics, *as currently structured and conducted* is not meeting the purposes for which it became a part of higher education. That being the case, we have a responsibility to dramatically restructure Division I athletics to do so or, if that proves impossible, eliminate it. The history of American higher education offers many examples of programs or departments that were downsized or eliminated when it became apparent that they had become obsolete, had failed to meet their purpose, or had become a drain on institutional resources.

That said, the root cause of college athletics' ills is not commercialism nor academic fraud but rather the model—the professional sports model—that higher education has chosen to meet its business, education, and commercial goals. Professional athletics is simply not an appropriate business for higher education.

In short, it is time to take a new road; a road that would require not simply strengthening eligibility standards but deconstructing the entire enterprise. Rather than trying to be all things to all people, higher education's responsibility in the cultural area of athletics should be twofold: first, to involve the maximum number of students in sports activities that can be enjoyed for a lifetime for purposes of promoting public health and, second, to provide entertaining but educationally based intercollegiate athletics.

Specifically, the professional model of intercollegiate athletics must be dismantled and rebuilt, not as a mirror of professional sports but in the image of an educational institution. To do so, the fundamental principle on which the professional sports model is built—pay for play—must be changed. Specifically, the athletic scholarship must be eliminated in favor of institutional, need-based aid.

Realizing change of this magnitude will be neither quick nor easy. It is, however, necessary. The higher education community must come together in a show of courage and confidence to halt the steady and destructive march of the win-at-any-cost professional model of intercollegiate athletics. It will require the courage and will of higher education leaders to act upon the fact that college athletics is higher education's property; not ESPN's or CBS's, not Nike's or Adidas's, not corporate America's, not the sports talk-show hosts', and not the crazed fan's in the stands. Because athletics is higher education's property, it is the higher education community alone that must establish the rules of the game, the values of the enterprise, and the principles upon which it will be presented to the public. The fact is, higher education leaders can make athletics look like and represent whatever they want. If these leaders are serious about reforming athletics, they must address the professional aspects of the enterprise.

It is important to note that calls to eliminate the athletic scholarship in favor of need-based aid are not new. The 1952 Special Committee on Athletic Reform of the American Council on Education recommended that scholarships be awarded based solely on academic need and academic ability rather than athletic ability. In 1989 the NCAA

Presidents Commission placed a proposal to establish a need-based aid system for all sports with the exception of football and basketball, plus two other women's sports selected by the institution. This proposal was withdrawn in favor of a resolution to study the issue further. And, more recently, the faculty-led Drake Group proposed a change to a need-based aid system as part of its reform agenda in 2001.

While some may interpret these failed attempts to adopt the need-based aid model as evidence that it will never pass, an alternative view would be that it is an idea whose time has yet to come. As mentioned, the changed context within which the ongoing reform movement is being played out offers a much more fertile environment for this idea to take root. But before this notion can gain traction, it will require a fundamental change in the collective mindset of the higher education and college athletics communities in three key ways: first, acknowledging that athletic scholarships are not in the best long-term educational interest of the athlete, second, acknowledging and effectively managing commercialism, and, third, debunking the "quality of game" myth.

FREEDOM TO PURSUE AN EDUCATION

At first glance, it would appear that eliminating athletic scholarships in favor of a need-based formula would not be in the best interest of student-athletes. However, if this proposal is judged upon what is in their best interest for the next fifty years of their lives, rather than the four or five years they are on campus, it becomes clear that eliminating the athletic grant will contribute significantly to athletes' chances of obtaining a well-balanced academic, personal, and athletic experience while in college.

An athletic scholarship represents a contractual agreement between the athlete and the coach, which allows coaches to view athletes as employees, bought and paid for by the athletics department. Thus, for many coaches, the scholarship has little to do with educational opportunity or financial need and everything to do with control. Athletic scholarships are a powerful means of keeping athletes focused upon athletic performance. If the athlete does not do what the coach wants, he can be "fired" because the athletic scholarship is a one-year agreement, renewable at the discretion of the coach.

A need-based financial aid agreement, however, is a contractual agreement between the student and the institution. It guarantees that the student will continue to receive his or her financial aid regardless of what transpires on the athletic fields. There is no more effective way to empower the athlete because it fundamentally changes the relationship between the athlete, the coach, and the institution. Under such a contract, the student is less beholden to the athletics department's competitive and business motives and thus freer to explore the wide diversity of experiences college offers.

Critics will argue that athletes are already underpaid in relation to the amount of money they generate for the institution. In the current professional model, college athletes *are* underpaid. The NCAA differentiates its "employment" arrangement from the professional model by claiming that the "student-athlete's" compensation is in the form of an "educational opportunity." Regrettably, in far too many cases, this "educational opportunity" is a sham. Despite all the attempts at academic reform, the current, professional model of college athletics has evolved to a point where the barriers to earning that well-balanced educational experience have become too great. It is no wonder athletes feel they are underpaid. They are clearly not getting the deal that was sold to them when the coach sat in their living rooms and promised a quality, well-balanced, academic, social, and athletic experience. In the need-based financial aid model, a legitimate educational experience is, once again, a viable part of the compensation package. And the value of a well-rounded, academically rigorous, and hard-earned educational experience is priceless.

Even NCAA president Myles Brand acknowledges that academic reform is not the central issue in changing the system to allow athletes to obtain a genuine educational opportunity. In discussing the latest series of academic reforms and graduation rates, he commented, "It's more complicated than just graduation rates. They are important and that's one good measure. But they don't cut to the heart of the problem. The heart of the problem is ensuring that student-athletes have a genuine opportunity for a first class education. That there are no artificial barriers put in their way by the system, by coaches—anything at all that prevents them, not just from taking courses, but getting a real education" (Rhoden, 2004, p. C-17–C-18).

Further, the financial hardship on athletes resulting from the shift to a need-based aid system will be less than one might think. While many football and basketball athletes will be required to pay a portion of their educational expenses, those who qualify for "full need" will receive it. Almost all other sports operate on what is known as an equivalency system, where most receive only partial athletic scholarships.

Besides, most college athletes do not play for the money. This point was eloquently stated by NCAA president Myles Brand in his 2005 "State of the Association Address" in describing the principle of amateurism:

> Amateurism is not about how much; it is about why. It is not about the money; it is about the motivation. The collegiate model—with amateurism as only part of it—is based on the idea that students come to college to get an education, and some of them—the most gifted and most determined—play sports under the banner of the university for the love of the game. As old fashioned as that may sound, I challenge the cynics to survey the 360,000 student-athletes who participate in college sports to see if they don't overwhelmingly say that is exactly why they play. . . .
> Amateurism has never been about the size of budgets or salaries. It isn't about facility expansion, or skyboxes or commercialism. Amateurism is about why student-athletes play sports. And that we should never change. (Brand, 2005b, p. A-4)

Brand is correct regarding why the vast majority of college athletes play sports. He is mistaken, however, in that once athletic scholarships began to be awarded, the amateur model did change. It became professional. In short, when you are paid to play, everything takes a back seat to athletic performance and expectations. The athlete knows it. The coach knows it. Everyone who watches knows it. So why do our educational institutions continue to sponsor, even celebrate, an arrangement that undermines a young person's ability to earn what is supposed to be an educational institution's most important and valuable commodity—a degree? It is time to acknowledge that it is the professional model, with the athletic scholarship at its foundation, that is the biggest barrier to athletes getting a genuine educational opportunity.

Another important rule change that would help in the transition of the current professional model to an educationally centered operation is eliminating freshman eligibility. The traditional argument for such a change has been that freshmen need the year away from high-pressure, big-time athletics to adjust academically and socially. While this argument remains valid, there is a far more important reason to initiate it.

Specifically, the inability to receive a full-ride athletic scholarship, coupled with having to sit out of competition as a freshman, will drive all but those who are serious about being genuine students from college programs. And there is absolutely nothing wrong with that. Athletes who will go to school only if they receive a full ride and play immediately can pursue their athletic career through the club system or with a professional team. If at some point these changes shock the system into becoming more balanced and educationally focused, reinstituting freshman eligibility could be considered. But a shock is what the current system needs, and the combination of these two changes will provide it.

Many will be unable to get beyond the impact these changes will have on the elite athlete, with the question being where they will go to hone their athletic skills. In our sports-obsessed culture, there is little doubt their needs will be met. The fact is, for too long the American system of athletics has catered to the narrow needs of a few elite athletes while shortchanging the vast majority of participants. While catering to the elite athlete might be appropriate for a club or professional team or league, it is inappropriate for an educational institution. The elite athlete will continue to flourish, as an alternative system or structure with highly competitive outlets to develop their athletic potential will surface.

In many sports, this shift is occurring already. The most obvious example is baseball, with its well-established minor league system. Interestingly, in the shadow of the minor league system, college baseball thrives. In soccer, tennis, swimming, and basketball, club sports are emerging to cater to the athletic needs of the elite. In basketball, the National Basketball Association (NBA) has established a developmental league with a minimum age limit of eighteen. Thus, a high school athlete, rather than attending college to refine his skills for the NBA, could move directly to the developmental league and proceed on to the NBA at age nineteen.

In short, the purpose of an educational institution should be more focused on providing legitimate educational opportunities for students who are interested in using athletics to supplement the educational process rather than elite athletes who view their stay on campus simply as a means of getting to the pros.

Besides, how much can athletes who are in school primarily to play sports really learn if they view college as nothing more than a way station on their steady march to the pros? Should we be wasting tax dollars and school resources on those who have little desire to learn? And why do we believe that college is for everyone or that if you want a college degree you must earn it by age twenty-two?

In the final analysis, a need-based aid system will help ensure a genuine, well-balanced educational experience for the athlete that offers far more long-term value than an athletic scholarship system that serves as a barrier to achieving a genuine educational experience. The fact is, receiving need-based aid resulting in a legitimate educational experience that leads to a meaningful degree is a far better deal than getting an athletic scholarship to cover the cost of an educational experience that is a sham.

Some argue that eliminating athletic scholarships and making freshmen ineligible will deny opportunity and limit access for many students, most notably, black athletes. The question is access to what? To the fields of competition or to a quality, well-balanced opportunity to earn a meaningful degree? With black basketball and football players generally graduating in the mid 30 to mid 40 percent range, respectively, earning an athletic scholarship under the current system is little more than an opportunity to play ball.

Given these results, the larger question is whether the athletic scholarship, and the tremendous influence coaches have over the athlete who receives one, serves to limit the ability of the athlete to have a well-balanced collegiate experience and earn a meaningful degree. After all, coaches are paid to win. As a result, their short-term interests (win next week's game) are often at odds with the athletes' long-term educational interests (earn a degree). This is simply the reality of the current system. How many more athletes would graduate if it were not for the excessive time, energy, physical, and emotional demands placed upon them from the athletics department; demands that, if not met, will result in the elimination of the scholarship? Rather than the athletic scholarship being the determining factor in earning a degree, it is more likely that athletes graduate in spite of the demands of being beholden to what amounts to a professional sports franchise. These young people are so motivated, smart, and determined, they will find a way to graduate with a need-based aid package as opposed to a full athletic scholarship.

Further, the athletic scholarship has made our educational institutions complicit in perpetuating a dangerous and counterproductive cultural myth. Specifically, far too many parents and youngsters believe sports, rather than education, is the ticket to future success. The professional model of college sports reinforces the myth that the road to economic and personal prosperity is best attained by chasing athletic fame, glory, and financial reward rather than by obtaining a quality education. This impact is particularly prevalent in the black community. One only has to consider the previously mentioned NCAA graduation rates to realize that, in most cases, this is a cruel hoax. While moving to a club system for elite athletics may not significantly change this myth, one thing is certain: our educational institutions should have absolutely no part in perpetuating it.

While the argument that the elimination of the athletic scholarship will inhibit some black athletes' ability to access higher education is powerful, a more likely result of this change will be that these black athletes will simply be replaced by other black athletes. While they may be a bit less talented and obsessed with athletics, they will likely be better students or at least more interested in academic achievement than in using the university as a springboard to the pros. In the end, more athletes, black, white, and Hispanic, will obtain a well-balanced college experience resulting in graduation.

What about those athletes who will not play for a school unless they receive a full ride and play as freshmen? Let them play elsewhere. The game and the institution will survive, as will the athletes' careers, as private sports clubs and pro leagues will create participation opportunities for those elite athletes to continue to hone their skills.

Not only would a need-based approach save money for our deficit-ridden athletics programs, it would bring the student-athlete ideal closer to a reality. Such a change would also have a significant public relations impact. The cynicism associated with the term *student-athlete* is widespread. Everyone knows the score. Many Division I participants are on campus to play ball, first and foremost. It is for this reason that the Drake Group has as one of its primary reform initiatives the elimination of the term *student-athlete*.

In keeping with higher education's responsibility to provide educational leadership in our society, the elimination of athletic scholarships will have a tremendous impact beyond the walls of academe. As chronicled daily in our newspapers, high school and youth programs have become increasingly competitive and pressure-packed: coaches screaming at seven-year-olds for committing an error and parents attacking Little League umpires, fighting at youth hockey practice, pushing their children to specialize in a sport at earlier and earlier ages, and suing coaches because their child does not get enough playing time. Much of this out-of-control behavior is justified in that it is the price necessary to earn a college scholarship which might then lead to a pro contract.

In addition to the elimination of the athletic scholarship and freshman eligibility, there are other aspects of the current college sports operation that must be changed. Spring football and other out-of-season practices should be eliminated, as should off-campus recruiting. Basketball and football coaching staffs should be cut in half. Seasons should be shortened, schedules reduced, and travel more restricted. The NCAA should also seek a Congressional antitrust exemption with regard to coaches' salaries to keep them more in line with faculty pay rather than Hollywood movie stars'. Simply put, it is a harmful example of misplaced educational values when the highest paid institutional employee is a coach. And to think that the public does not notice these warped priorities is naïve.

These changes will significantly shrink the size, budgets, and campus influence of athletics departments. They address the major areas where the athletics "arms race" proliferates: recruiting, salaries, size of staff, and travel. In short, if you operate a business where expenses outpace revenue, and will continue to do so in the future (How many more stadium boxes can you build and how much more stadium signage can you sell?), there is only one way to become solvent: cut expenses and overhead. Shrink the operation.

Another argument against eliminating athletic scholarships in favor of need-based, institutional financial aid is that such a change will open the door for schools to gain a competitive advantage by constructing "creative" need packages and offering better paying jobs. This is an example of the way in which the current professional model, and the attitudes and concerns it spurs, has resulted in the creation of an enterprise that has become divorced from sound academic values and principles. The fear that a particular change will result in a competitive advantage or disadvantage or an increase in cheating is simply not an acceptable excuse for opposing rules that are in the best long-term educational and personal interests of the student. For too long, the driving force behind the creation of rules has been the fear and paranoia of coaches and administrators and the operating principles of the professional model rather than the best, long-term academic interests of the students.

Rules should be adopted with the assumption that they will be followed rather than circumvented or ignored. As with any rule, there exists the potential for abuse. Those who will abuse a new rule are likely the same people who have been abusing the current rules. One of the great injustices in college athletics is that rules have become far too restrictive, penalizing the majority for the misdeeds of the few. Change that will benefit the majority of students and coaches should not be scrapped simply because of the paranoia of a few and the dishonesty of even fewer.

That said, today's compliance systems are significantly more effective at monitoring financial aid abuse. Twenty years ago, the Presidents Commission challenged the NCAA and its member institutions to develop and implement programs to ensure more effective institutional control of athletics programs and operations. The NCAA has responded to that challenge. While not perfect or foolproof, schools have invested in compliance programs to the point where the framework of a system of checks and balances is in place. It is time to allow and trust that system to do its work.

According to Brand, the NCAA is poised to increase its enforcement efforts to hold the few dishonest ones accountable: "Will people cheat? Probably. They do now. There is pressure to do so now. Does that mean we shouldn't set new rules and enforce them? My expectation is that our members will rise to the occasion. And we've increased our enforcement staff by 50 percent. When you break the rules, we'll nail you" (qtd. in Pennington, 2004, p. C-17).

Yes, there will be abuses, but that possibility exists with any rule. But if the athletic scholarship and the professional model it has resulted in has become the biggest barrier students face in obtaining a well-balanced educational experience, why should they be penalized because the "adults" associated with the enterprise can not trust each other?

There is, however, a far more insidious reason for resisting the elimination of the athletic scholarship. As mentioned, the deeper concern of coaches and administrators is loss of control. Most coaches would rather provide a full athletic scholarship, not because they are concerned about the athletes' financial well being but because the scholarship locks the athlete into the professional, pay-for-play model. For the vast majority of athletes, however, such a change will release them from what often amounts to excessive athletics department influence and oversight. The increased independence that will result from these changes will enhance their ability to achieve a well-balanced athletic, academic, and social experience and better prepare them to function as responsible citizens after their playing days are over. Athletic scholarships only reinforce the myth that the road to economic and personal prosperity is best attained by chasing athletic fame, glory, and wealth rather than by obtaining a quality education.

In the final analysis, if we have the long-term academic and personal interests of young people in mind, the athletic scholarship should be eliminated in favor of a system that assures them a legitimate opportunity to actualize the personal, academic, athletic, and economic opportunities afforded by a well-balanced college education. Specifically, our policies and daily actions must show very clearly that education is the primary purpose of our athletics departments and that the true measure of success hinges upon obtaining a degree.

There is another aspect of the current professional model that must be changed. At far too many Division I schools, the athletics department operates as a separate, stand-alone entity. If the point of athletics reform is to more effectively integrate the athletics department into the mainstream of the institution, a crucial step to that end is to structurally integrate the athletics department into the institutional administrative structure.

For example, sports information and marketing departments should be moved from under direct athletics department control. One of the primary justifications for incorporating athletics into higher education was that its visibility could be used to promote the virtues of the school to a wider audience. It is debatable, however, whether these departments have done an effective job of promoting educational themes. This failure is not because the individuals in these departments are incapable of weaving educational messages into their publications and programs. Rather, because they are housed in, and employed by, the athletics department, their directive has been to promote athletics. Moving the authority for the promotional arms of the athletics department to the university's office of institutional advancement would better serve the interests of the institution. Although the promotional materials produced and activities conducted would not change overnight, as a result of being exposed to institutional influences and being held directly accountable to the office of institutional advancement, over time, institutional messages and themes would be woven into athletics promotions.

A similar case can be made for incorporating the athletics fundraising operation into the university's office of institutional advancement. Once again, a primary justification for the incorporation of athletics into higher education was that it would contribute to the institution's efforts to raise the resources necessary for survival. Those resources took the form of money from alumni, the corporate community, and other interested parties, as well as the political favor of state legislators. But, here again, these promises have been largely unmet due to the isolation of the athletics department from the mainstream campus community.

Integrating the athletics department marketing and fundraising operations into the university's office of institutional advancement would not mean that efforts to promote or raise money for the athletics department would be discontinued. Rather, those efforts would continue as part of university-wide efforts to generate publicity and resources. If a fundamental justification for athletics is that it generates exposure and resources for the university, then all efforts related to these functions should be subject to the direct oversight and control of the university's office of institutional advancement. Despite the claim from athletics department officials that they work closely with the university's office of institutional advancement, given the separation and mistrust that exists between most athletics departments and the rest of the academic community, such cooperation is generally superficial and must improve significantly if higher education is to fully tap athletics' potential to contribute to its mission.

Further, the athletics department should be included as a line item in the university's budget. Direct university governance over athletics department budgets would have many benefits. Such oversight would bring a higher level of fiscal control and would allow closer institutional examination of athletics department programs and objectives. It would also send a clear message that athletics has important enough educational value for it to be fully incorporated into the financial workings of the institution rather than that it has solely economic value, as is suggested by a separate financial process. Finally, it would enable the university to determine exactly how much of an investment it wishes to make in athletics.

The most effective way in which to integrate the athletics program into the mainstream university administrative and governance structure would be to do as Vanderbilt University did in 2004. Rather than taking a piecemeal approach, President Gordon Gee, with the support of his board of trustees, placed Vanderbilt's athletics department under the umbrella of the Division of Student Life and University Affairs. By fully integrating the athletics department into the university's administrative and governance structure, he made the very profound statement that the athletics department is meant to be a part of, rather than apart from, the institution and that the institution's parts will act as one. While there was an initial uproar over the change, the Vanderbilt community has adjusted and the university is moving forward—as one.

Traditionally, reform efforts have been directed at academics, specifically the raising of eligibility standards. Most recently, the NCAA refined its approach to academic reform with the adoption of an "incentives/disincentives" plan that will penalize schools whose athletes fail to meet specific academic standards. Penalties include the reduction of athletic scholarships and eventual disqualification from NCAA postseason play. This plan is significant in that, for the first time, team, coach, and institutional accountability are considered. To date, the only individual who paid a real price for academic failure was the athlete. Meanwhile, the coach, team, and institution escaped unscathed, regardless of the role they played in the athlete's failure.

While the new approach may help, the fact is, academic reform will not fundamentally alter the Division I landscape. Raising academic standards does not mainstream athletes as intended. Rather, these changes result in a greater dependence on athletics department tutoring services, the creation of pseudo-majors to keep athletes eligible, and an "arms race" in the area of academic support programs.

While holding coaches and programs more directly accountable is the most promising aspect of this new approach, it is also its biggest drawback. To date, the only individual held accountable for academic failure has been the athlete. While a coach or a team might be impacted when an athlete is forced to leave school, the coach and the team, for the most part, survive and move on. Even so, academic fraud has flourished. Arguably, under this new approach, the pressure to commit academic fraud will intensify significantly because the coach and his or her program will be directly and immediately impacted by an athlete's failure to make academic progress. In other words, the stakes for coaches have been raised. As a result, the pressure and propensity to cheat has been raised as well.

That aside, as long as athletes are getting paid to play, the professional model, complete with its escalating budgets, widening deficits, and attendant public skepticism, will remain. While raising academic standards will result in a few more athletes graduating, the fundamental underpinnings, culture, and operating principles of the professional system will remain.

ACKNOWLEDGING AND MANAGING COMMERCIALISM

Concern regarding the impact of commercialism on academic and institutional values is not limited to athletics. Facing formidable fiscal challenges on many fronts, colleges and universities have had to adopt new strategies and behaviors more conducive to revenue enhancement and more responsive to an increasingly competitive higher education marketplace. To that end, institutions have been aggressively searching for ways to partner with the corporate community to advance their mission. As Derek Bok writes

in *Universities in the Marketplace* (2003), "Entrepreneur-
ship is no longer the exclusive province of athletics departments and development offices; it has taken hold in science
faculties, business schools, continuing education divisions,
and other academic units across the campus" (p. 3).

There are, however, challenges associated with higher
education's embrace of commercial opportunities. Cynthia
Patterson, vice president for academic affairs at Fischer
College, outlined them in *Sports in Schools: The Future of
an Institution* (2000):

> As institutional decision making was refined in terms of
> revenue enhancement and responses to the demands of
> the marketplace, the norms and values of higher educa-
> tion shifted away from mission and purpose. Educational
> priorities were no longer immune from the vicissitudes of
> the marketplace. Consequently, colleges and universities
> found themselves struggling to find ways to respond to the
> realities of the marketplace without destroying the values,
> ideals, and purposes that remained essential to both their
> missions as educational institutions and their responsibili-
> ties as democratic institutions. For higher education leaders,
> the lines of distinction between "good business" and "good
> education" were becoming increasingly blurred. (p. 122)

These are challenges that athletics departments have
been wrestling with for years. Many claim that athletics
has already sold its soul to the "Gods of Commercialism
and Television." While that may be true to some extent, the
reforms suggested here present an opportunity for athletics to recalibrate its relationship to the corporate and television communities. The question is how best to manage
athletics' commercialism to maximize its contribution to
broader institutional mission.

The current relationship between commercialization and athletics is clearly a case where the sum of the whole is far greater than the parts. Rampant commercialism, coupled with a product with values that are blatantly hypocritical, offers up a combination that is particularly insidious. The use of athletics for commercial purposes would be much more palatable if the product being sold was being driven by educational, rather than professional athletics, values and priorities.

This is not to say that when universities reject the professional model the negative impact of excessive commercialization will disappear. Nor does it mean that universities should not seek to exploit commercial markets for greater educational and institutional advantage. Rather, given its place as a public institution, higher education must be more sensitive and judicious in tapping those commercial opportunities.

In other words, the fact that our colleges and universities should not be sponsoring professional athletics franchises does not mean that intercollegiate athletics, or even commercialized athletics, should be eliminated from higher education. On the contrary, the benefits and positive influence of university-sponsored athletics programs that are operated in a fiscally sound and academically responsible manner can be enormous. Such programs, even programs with commercial ties, can advance an academic agenda and contribute to institutional mission in meaningful ways.

Although these concepts appear to be contradictory, they are not. While both the professional sports model and commercialization impact the institution, it is the values, priorities, pressures, and general environment associated with the professional model that pollutes the higher education well.

Commercialism is unavoidably linked to sports sponsorship at any level. But it is a by-product that can be managed. There is, however, no managing the professional model. The expectations and values of the professional model are very clear to all involved: pay for play. The athlete either gets paid—whether in the form of cash or a scholarship—or he doesn't. And the receipt of that compensation is dependent on one thing—performance on the fields of play. If the athlete does not perform athletically, he or she is often asked to leave the team, which, in most cases, results in the athlete leaving school.

The standard for remaining in an educational institution, however, should always be based on academics rather than athletics. This fundamental difference in performance standard is why the professional model and its expectations and values are simply not compatible with the values and purpose of the academic institution.

Proof of the conflicting values of these two cultures lies in the NCAA manual. NCAA rules are so complex, convoluted, and, all too often, outright absurd because of the inherent hypocrisy of the system. It is precisely because of the extreme disconnect between the values of the professional sports model and educational institutions that such an elaborate set of rules and regulations is necessary. The NCAA manual is an attempt to reconcile these two extremely different value systems and cultures. The five hundred pages of NCAA rules are necessary to perpetuate the illusion of a professional sports model being "about education." The fact is, coaches, particularly in the revenue-generating sports, no longer buy into the NCAA's academic model because they view their relationship with the individuals in their charge, not as a teacher-student relationship but rather as a coach-athlete relationship. While they, for appearance' sake, talk about the teacher-student relationship, they know that the athletic scholarship makes the relationship an athletic contract. Athletes know this as well. Coaches' pay offers another example of this fundamental disconnect. The hypocrisy is striking when a coach's salary is double that of the institution's president. With the elimination of the foundation upon which the professional model is based, the pay-for-play, athletic scholarship arrangement, the hypocrisy and competing values and culture that the system is trying to reconcile and keep a lid on, disappears.

Sports advocates will claim that these standards do not have to be mutually exclusive. They believe that an athlete can perform both on the fields of play and in the classroom. They are correct. There are many who do meet this dual challenge. The problem, however, is that the demands of the professional model are increasingly making this goal unrealistic. While well intentioned, attempts by the NCAA to make these competing demands more balanced and manageable have largely been ineffective.

From television's influence over starting times of games, to shoe companies supplementing coaches' contracts, to corporate logos plastered on fields and scoreboards, there is no denying that college athletics is impacted by an enormous corporate influence. But simply because corporate influence is prevalent does not necessarily mean it is the big, bad ogre of college sports. Commercialism has become an easy target, primarily because it implies that the problems of college athletics result from external influences.

This analysis of these ills is convenient because it places the responsibility for the evolution of the enterprise on outside influences rather than decades of a lack of engagement and resolve on the part of faculty, presidents, and trustees.

The following concepts bear mentioning again. Athletics was incorporated into higher education primarily for financial and commercial reasons. Given the changing economic realities of higher education funding, athletics' revenue and public relations potential will become increasingly important. And there is nothing inherently wrong with higher education running athletics as a business provided it is a business that is appropriate for higher education.

Commercialism can add educational value if managed properly. The challenge is to manage this resource to meet the rapidly changing fiscal, community-building, and public relations needs of the university. Central to that challenge is the recognition of two facts. First, we must accept the notion that as long as we have athletics, commercialism will be a part of it. The genie of commercialism has long been out of the bottle and will never return to it. Second, we must also recognize that the financing of American higher education is radically different from such financing twenty years ago. Presidents are becoming less academic leaders than businessmen and fundraisers as colleges have become major financial engines. From corporate naming rights for business schools to corporate-sponsored research, the commercialism of higher education is here to stay. Given a future economic outlook of increasing costs and declining revenues and state funding, the pressure on institutions to partner with commercial entities to maintain academic excellence while balancing budgets will only increase. Against this backdrop, the commercialism of athletics will look increasingly less radical and out of line with the financing of higher education generally.

In this environment, athletics' potential to generate resources becomes increasingly important. At issue is not whether athletics can or should be used as a commercial entity to advance institutional mission but rather how to construct and operate the enterprise to maximize its commercial and educational value while minimizing its propensity to undermine academic values and drain institutional resources. The fundamental question regarding this challenge is whether the professional model, with its runaway costs, continued undermining of academic integrity, and win-at-all-costs culture is the most effective way to achieve these ends.

Regardless of the form athletics assumes, the commercial aspect of the operation must be effectively managed and, in some very important ways, limited. For example, college athletics' relationship with television must be reconsidered. There are too many games on television on weekdays and many of these games begin too late. The only reason for starting late is television. While coaches and athletes love playing on television, these are school nights. My two children often beg to stay up past their bedtime on a school night. Do I let them? No. By sticking to my principles, they will (hopefully) begin to understand that school is their most important priority.

Does this mean that weekday, televised games should be eliminated? No. If conferences and television networks become more flexible and creative, they can meet the majority of each other's concerns. For example, they can agree that televised games during the week can only occur between teams that are less than two hundred miles apart. Further, those games could begin by 7:00 PM. This would allow the students (in the new model they would be first and foremost students rather than athletes) to return to campus at a reasonable hour for school the following day. While this will present scheduling challenges for conferences, they can be overcome with commitment, creativity, and cooperation.

Some argue that such restrictions would result in a significant loss of revenue from television contracts. That does not necessarily have to be the case. Under such a system, television networks would continue to be able to meet the vast majority of their programming needs. For example, while East Coast games would not be able to fill the current 9:00 PM EST time slot, Midwest and West Coast games could. Yes, the West Coast might be left in the dark for the 9:00 PM PST time slot, but that is a small price to pay for a change that would send a clear signal that college athletics is truly about education. Along the way, the commercial value of the enterprise will actually be enhanced as corporations and the public want to be associated with entities that are viewed as positive and educational rather than hypocritical.

The fact is, college athletics, the television networks, and the public will survive without college games on television seven nights a week and without 9:00 PM local games on the West Coast. While this is only one suggestion to manage the commercial aspect of the postprofessional model, the point is that, with a little creativity and flexibility, television's demand for programming, the academic needs of the students, and the institution's mission can be met more effectively.

DEBUNKING THE "QUALITY OF GAME" MYTH

Somewhere along the line we have bought into a notion advanced by the athletics community that what makes college athletics commercially viable is the "quality of the game." This has lead to a drive to mirror professional sports training, playing, and behavioral and management styles in every way possible. This mentality has driven the cost structure of our programs to a point that no longer makes sense. Nevertheless, the mere suggestion of the progressive reforms in this book will result in claims from coaches and athletics directors that the public will not accept the diminished "quality of game" that might result from such changes.

How do they know?

There is absolutely no evidence to suggest progressive change would adversely affect the University of Florida's, Pennsylvania State University's, or the University of California, Los Angeles's long-term sports entertainment value in the marketplace. Ultimately, the University of Alabama fan who is watching the running back turn the corner to score a touchdown does not care whether that youngster runs the forty-yard dash in 4.4 or 4.8 seconds, or whether he participated in spring practice, or whether he is on an athletic scholarship, or whether the coach visited him at his home to recruit him, or how much his coach is paid. That fan cares about only two things. First, whether Auburn University is abiding by the same rules and, second, whether the player scores a touchdown for Alabama.

It has been the athletics establishment's unyielding adherence to this notion of the "quality of the game," coupled with the academic community's lack of courage to confront their claims, that is most responsible for the fiscal excesses and professionalization of college athletics. College athletics' appeal rests not in how high the players jump or how fast they run but rather in the fact that the activity is steeped in university, educational, and cultural tradition. Michigan University-Ohio State University, University of Texas–Texas A&M University, Harvard University-Yale University, and Auburn-Alabama will always draw crowds, be covered by the media, and captivate the public's imagination, regardless of the level of play.

These sentiments have been echoed by journalists and television representatives on more than one occasion. During the January 23, 2001, meeting of the Knight Commission, Loren Matthews, senior vice president at ABC and former vice president at ESPN, testified on the role of television in college sports. During a discussion of the impact of increased academic standards on the quality of game, Matthews was asked whether he thought that "if the game was played at a less than professional level by real students that you (ABC) would drop college sports or would it still be valuable?"

Matthews responded,

> Just as it's difficult to compare the college or pro athlete
> from generation to generation, . . . if the level of play is
> consistent, . . . who's going to know the difference? . . .
> Some teams will still be better than others, but I don't know
> that the fan or we or anyone is sophisticated enough to
> say that the game is being played with six percent less effi-
> ciency than it was played with five years ago. . . . If you
> still had either scholarship athletes in total, at all participat-
> ing universities, or non-scholarship athletes participating

in all universities, there would still be a level of play that would be consistent across the board. I would think from a fan's end it would be an acceptable level. (Knight Foundation Commission on Intercollegiate Athletics, 2001b)

Mike Aresco, senior vice president for programming for CBS, was asked a similar question during a Knight Commission hearing on November 14, 2003: "We realize that in the end if we do not embrace amateurism we will not have a product that people want to watch. I think in the end, these are kids and people want to watch a kind of pure competition that they don't see at the pro level. If we lose that we're all in trouble."

Later in his testimony, Aresco commented on the impact of a series of academic reform measures that the NCAA was in the process of adopting:

We don't, despite what people may think, view that as in any way a threat to our product. We don't fear it at all. We think it is a good thing. We embrace it. We do not have a product in the end if our game is plagued by scandal. We don't have a product if people think that these kids are not even remotely academic students, that they are not near the classrooms. No one benefits from that. The feeling that we have to have a semi-pro league on the screen is not, is not the case. We were asked, when I appeared before the Knight Commission before, at what level is there a dilution in talent that really affects what you can televise? We are so far from that point because we have already seen most of our top players leave for the NBA and it has not affected, in the end, the quality of what we put on the air. We still have a vibrant, terrific tournament. (Knight Foundation Commission on Intercollegiate Athletics, 2003)

Or, in the words of *New York Times* columnist William Rhoden (2005), describing why he was such a fan of North Carolina State University basketball player Julius Hodge: "I'm not a Julius Hodge fan because he hit a game winning shot or scored 17 points or passed for 6 assists yesterday. I am a fan because he has been able to maintain focus on his classes and his college life" (p. D-1).

In short, if higher education wishes to maximize athletics' commercial potential, higher education leaders must be smart about the type of "business" they run. The key to a successful athletic entertainment business is maintaining public interest. Public perception of your "brand," or what your business stands for and is about, is critical. Like it or not, due to the dominance of Division I basketball and football in the media and public consciousness, the current NCAA brand does not stand for students pursuing an education but rather for pampered, mercenary athletes who have little interest in attending class and are using college as a vehicle for getting to the pros.

It is important to recognize how this brand or public perception will impact the business. The closer college athletics moves towards the professional model, the less distinct it becomes from the NBA or National Football League (NFL). The result is an increase in the number of people who will become cynical and fed up with the hypocrisy of our colleges and universities saying that college athletics is "about education" while knowing it is being run like a professional sports franchise. As the NCAA brand becomes less distinct, more people will lose interest in the "product."

Derek Bok (2003), president emeritus of Harvard University, writes,

Intercollegiate athletics cannot attract large revenues without sustaining the perception, valid or not, that the players really *are* students. Once this perception vanishes, the magic disappears. College teams become mere minor league clubs, few of which have ever won large public followings or elicited much interest from television audiences. Before long, the system would collapse, and university officials would have to acknowledge an uncomfortable truth. Educational institutions have absolutely no business operating farm systems for the benefit of the National Football League and the National Basketball Association. (pp. 124–25)

Hard-core sports fans will never turn off college games, regardless of how professional. For the same reason, these fans will continue to follow college sports regardless of whether or not the players receive scholarships. But there are many other less hard-core fans that have already or will walk away from the hypocrisy if the product looks too much like the professional model. Rejecting the professional model would ensure that the college athletics brand remains distinct from the professional sports brand. As a result, the public would be more likely to continue to support college sports or, for those who have become disenchanted, to reconnect with it.

Again, it is not inherently inappropriate for higher education to operate athletics as a business, unless the product undermines the core purpose of the institution. There are plenty of examples of businesses that have eliminated departments or operations that were underperforming or were no longer in harmony with the fundamental business purposes.

Similarly, a department that operates on core principles that are diametrically opposed to those of the education community should not be sponsored by a college or university. Less can be more. Downsizing or eliminating a failed unit or product will improve efficiency and strengthen a business's ability to meet its core objectives. The core business of a university is education. The fundamental operating principle of the professional sports model is to provide entertainment and generate profit on the backs of pay-for-play athletes. By eliminating the pay-for-play agreement, American higher education will eliminate its departments of professional athletics and all they represent. This will allow athletics departments to restructure their operations and refocus their energies to contribute more effectively to higher education's core purpose of education.

Despite the self-serving rhetoric of coaches and athletics administrators, the popularity of college athletics is not driven by the requirement that it mirror the professional sports model. To the contrary, college athletics' appeal rests in the notion that it stands for something other than a win-at-all-costs business enterprise where athletes are cogs in a machine with no other purpose than to win games, generate revenue, and provide entertainment. What makes college athletics attractive is that there is a link to a higher purpose, specifically, education. In college, athletes are supposed to be students; coaches are supposed to be educators; and the games, above all, are supposed to be about school spirit and fun.

While we tend to focus on the commercial and financial impact of athletics on broader institutional goals, the most important and powerful potential benefit athletics offers higher education is public exposure and visibility. This is why maintaining a brand that is clearly distinct from the professional model is so critical. Athletics is by far the largest and clearest window through which the public views the university. According to an NCAA-sponsored survey, 53 percent of the total American public, 65 percent of men and 43 percent of women, follow college sports (NCAA, 1991, p. 22).

Regrettably, that visibility has been used almost exclusively to promote athletics rather than education. In short, college sports is packaged, marketed, and projected as purely entertainment. Given the current professional model, it is easy to understand how universities have missed these opportunities to use athletics to advance larger institutional purposes. The management of athletics programs, particularly in areas pertaining to television and radio broadcast rights and negotiations, has always been left to athletics directors and conference commissioners. Given that these administrators are responsible for managing the professional sports model, they simply have not considered control over the content of those broadcasts as a means of promoting educational goals to be an issue of primary importance. But they cannot be blamed, because university administrators have not fully appreciated the tremendous opportunity televised games provide to effectively promote the value, mission, and goals of higher education. Corporate America has recognized the power of television to send messages and to project images to the public. That is why advertising agencies are paid millions of dollars to develop strategies for selling their clients' products or services. Higher education should seize the same opportunity to communicate its message and shape its image through telecasts of its athletic contests.

While the NCAA and conferences have become more effective in using their thirty-second promotional spots to promote educational themes, there remains a disconnect and credibility gap between those advertisements and what the public is viewing during the game. In short, it is difficult for the NCAA to credibly promote education when the product is professional sports played by mercenary athletes rather than "real student-athletes."

The effective use of athletics' widespread visibility and brand is becoming increasingly important for higher education. One of the greatest challenges facing educational leaders today is the task of maintaining public trust in higher education. To do so, higher education must become more effective in telling its story to the public. For example, one such story might be how the cancer research being conducted at Pennsylvania State University might one day save the life of a viewer's child. Another might be how research being conducted at Mississippi State University is helping farmers in the South use land more efficiently. Athletics, through its televised games and the many other ways that it interfaces with the public, present a tremendous opportunity for higher education to illustrate specifically how it contributes to improving the lives of individual citizens and to let people know that higher education is a resource available to all. Televised games, as higher education's most visible activity, must be used more effectively to further the goals of the university rather than the specific goals of the athletics department.

The elimination of the professional model will make it easier to project messages that are more compatible with educational values and institutional mission. Further, it will present the higher education community with a golden opportunity to reconsider and restructure all coverage of athletic events, from the content of commercial spots to the subjects discussed during halftime to pregame and coaches' shows and interviews in order to determine whether more effective use can be made of this valuable resource.

For example, thirty-second infomercials designed to inform prospective athletes of NCAA initial eligibility standards are often aired throughout games. This well-intentioned effort simply highlights the limited way in which television exposure has been used. These spots target only prospective athletes and not prospective students generally. Informing prospective athletes of NCAA eligibility standards is important, but informing all prospective students of admissions processes and financial aid opportunities would have a far broader and longer lasting impact on higher education.

Changing the foundation upon which college athletics rests will open opportunities to restructure television and radio broadcasts to more effectively contribute to the goals and mission of the institution. Other examples include increased influence in the selection and training of game announcers to ensure that they have some understanding of the goals and mission of higher education, not solely of the dynamics of the forward pass or jump shot. Announcers could be provided with information that would enable them, during timeouts, to interject a sound bite promoting an educational program or an accomplishment of one of the universities involved in the contest rather than a meaningless statistic about a long-forgotten guard on the 1923 championship team.

"Player of the Game" features could be eliminated in favor of segments that highlight student-athletes' accomplishments off the field. In an educationally centered model, such examples would be much easier to find. During time-outs, administrators of the institutions involved could provide information on their admissions and financial aid processes to encourage potential students and their parents to consider the college opportunities available. Providing more information on the process of applying to, and value of attending, college is becoming increasingly important as most high schools are woefully understaffed in the guidance counseling area.

While the purpose of these changes would not be to turn a televised college football game into a National Geographic special, eliminating the professional model of college sports would present a genuine opportunity for higher education to reconsider and restructure its relationship with television. The goal would be to weave educational messages and images throughout broadcasts more effectively and thus to utilize better athletics' tremendous potential to contribute to institutional mission in this important area.

For those who think that such a change in tenor and tone of broadcasts will drive television networks and the public away from televised sports, the fact is, television needs college athletics every bit as much as college athletics needs television. Networks must fill programming time. Network executives know that college sports sell. Televised college athletics is a hot property. The public wants to see it and will continue to watch it even if more time is carved out of broadcasts to promote educational themes. While the bright lights and cheering crowds of athletics is easier to package as exciting product, if half as much time and money were spent developing creative ways to advertise education as are now spent on promoting next week's "big games," creative and captivating sound bites, infomercials, and images about higher education might hold the attention of viewers otherwise inclined to channel surf or leave their sets to get a snack. And if one network did not appreciate higher education's need to project its successes more effectively, other networks will.

AN OPPORTUNITY TO REDO
THE EXPERIMENT

Because its most fundamental purpose is to provide educational, scientific, moral, medical, and ethical leadership in helping our society meet the many challenges it faces in today's rapidly changing, increasingly complex world, higher education must manage athletics with those purposes in mind. To this end, this important and extremely visible property must be conducted based upon sound educational principles rather than the values and operating standards of a professional sports franchise.

Higher education's experiment with elite athletics has failed. This failure to advance institutional purposes is a product of the model of athletics that higher education has chosen. The values and operating principles of the professional model are simply not compatible with the values and purposes of an academic institution. At the core of that model lies the athletic scholarship, a pay-for-play compensation arrangement that is based on athletic performance, with academic achievement an afterthought at best. That said, athletics is fully capable of complementing and contributing to an educational institution's mission in very timely and relevant ways if it is restructured with those purposes in mind.

Malcolm Gladwell, in *The Tipping Point*, describes that one dramatic moment or event in an epidemic or social movement when everything can change at once as the "tipping point." Higher education has been at the reform game, with limited success, for decades. That does not mean there has not been significant progress in building the foundation and critical mass that can serve as backdrop for significant change. As articulated in chapters 4 and 5, the foundation and critical mass necessary to support fundamental change is in place. All that is needed is the match to light the fire; the one event or initiative that begins the avalanche of change. That initiative is the elimination of the athletic scholarship.

The elimination of the athletic scholarship will provide American higher education with the much needed opportunity to recalibrate every aspect of its relationship with athletics. It will provide an opportunity to rewrite its chapter on athletics; to redo its experiment of using sports as a vehicle to advance educational goals and academic mission. But to do so, we must get beyond the fear that eliminating the athletic scholarship and the department of professional athletics would cause the entire enterprise to collapse. To the contrary, it would make it more educationally sound, more commercially viable, and, thus, more effective in contributing to larger university purposes.

Even if there were a negative impact on revenues and public interest in college athletics, it would be a small price to pay to remake college athletics in a way that would allow athletes to be genuine students, coaches to be true educators, and the athletics department to supplement, rather than undermine, academic values and institutional mission. More likely, however, such changes would increase college athletics' public appeal, as many who have lost interest in college athletics due to the hypocrisy inherent in the current system may regain respect for and interest in college sports. This is because most people want college athletics programs to stand for something more than simply turning a buck, preparing the next generation of professional stars, and winning at any cost. For these reasons, corporate interest in college athletics would also increase as companies prefer to associate their product with positive institutions.

Not only the public but also the corporate community and television networks would continue to be interested in and support college athletics, provided it resembles something distinct from professional sports. Because it is the only college game in town, people would continue to come to games, watch them on television, listen to them on radio, and read about them in the newspapers. But if it comes to resemble professional sports too closely, college athletics' unique niche in the marketplace will vanish. So why not spend less money on the enterprise and, in the process, reconnect it to the educational institution and academic values?

In the end, if the operation is downsized, deconstructed, and rebuilt on a sound educational foundation, not only will they continue to come, but many more will join them.

ARTICULATING AND MEETING RESPONSIBILITIES

You can't escape the responsibility of tomorrow by evading it today.

—Abraham Lincoln

There is a well-worn story about the doctor telling the patient, "I've got good news and bad news regarding your health." Well, here is the good news and bad news about the current health of college athletic reform.

First, the bad news.

Since 1982, when a group of presidents, working through the American Council on Education, proposed a set of academic standards that significantly raised the bar for freshman eligibility, higher education has been earnestly engaged in the issue of athletics reform. During this time, much progress has been made in student-athlete welfare, compliance, institutional control, and fiscal transparency.

Yet, despite this progress, in the most fundamental way, nothing has changed. The vast majority of Division I programs continue to lose money at an alarming rate and undermine academic values and institutional mission in significant ways. While much has been accomplished in reforming the structure, governance, and conduct of Division I athletics, the fact is that the higher education community has failed to honestly address its most fundamental flaw. Our colleges and universities continue to sponsor professional sports operations with core values and principles that are diametrically opposed to those of academic institutions. In short, American higher education has absolutely no business being in the business of professional athletics.

Despite a rash of scandals suggesting that reform is a lost cause, there is good news. The prescribed remedy is as clear as the illness: the elimination of the athletic scholarship as a way to de-professionalize the enterprise. And, as outlined in chapters 4 and 5, there is growing evidence that the table of reform may finally be set. We may be approaching the tipping point for revolutionary change provided we have the courage to pursue it.

Like the patient who must come to grips with his illness and develop the resolve and discipline to change his lifestyle to overcome it, so too must higher education. In other words, systemic reform is no longer a theoretical exercise; it now requires a choice. It is up to the patient to choose to do what is necessary to defeat the disease that has invaded his body.

This begs the following question for trustees, presidents, athletics administrators, athletes, coaches, and faculty members: Why is reform of the type advocated in this book in their interest and what can they do to advance that agenda?

IT'S ALL ABOUT INTEGRITY

Higher education's foundation rests upon public purpose. Thus, maintaining the public's trust is perhaps the most critical factor in higher education's remaining an important and relevant public institution. When its integrity is called into question or is compromised, the public loses confidence in higher education's ability to meet the many challenges facing our society. Thus, it is no surprise that the call to arms of the higher education community regarding athletics centers on the issue of integrity. In short, public confidence and trust is the lifeblood of an educational institution and every member of the higher education community should be concerned if any university operation, department, or function erodes that public confidence.

As articulated in the 1929 Carnegie Report and each of the Knight Commission reports, the responsibility for providing leadership regarding reform rests with presidents. But presidents will not be able to do it alone. As the 2001 Knight Commission report states, "Change will come, sanity will be restored, only when the higher education community comes together to meet collectively the challenges its members face" (Knight Foundation Commission on Intercollegiate Athletics, 2001a, p. 24).

With this in mind, the purpose of this chapter is twofold: first, to personalize the stakes involved in athletics reform for key constituent groups and, second, to provide a sense of what each constituent group can do to meet their responsibility to contribute to the growing critical mass for reform.

TRUSTEES: THE NEXUS BETWEEN THE PUBLIC AND THE INSTITUTION

It can no longer be denied that the way colleges and universities conduct their athletics programs has greatly contributed to our society's loss of perspective regarding the role that sports should play in our schools, communities, and culture. While this argument was advanced in chapter 2, it bears mentioning again because it is this loss of perspective and higher education's contribution to it that relates directly to trustees' reform responsibilities.

The primary responsibility of trustees is to serve as the nexus between the public and the institution. A major function in that regard is to identify societal issues and needs and then turn around and provide the leadership, vision, and framework to enable the institution to address those challenges. In meeting that charge, trustees must consider issues and challenges, not simply from the perspective of their particular institution or higher education generally, but from a larger societal perspective. This frame of reference should be no different for athletics.

Trustees have only recently been challenged to become more engaged in addressing athletics issues. Most notably, the Knight Commission in 2001 called on governing boards to work collaboratively with their chief executives to examine the place of intercollegiate athletics in the academy's hierarchy of values and mission. There appears to be some movement within the trustee community to initiate such an examination. For example, the Association of Governing Boards, the national membership organization for trustees, released a document in 2004 outlining guidelines for board governance in the area of intercollegiate athletics. Boards have been encouraged to use this document as a basis for discussion and as a primer for trustees, presidents, and other institutional leaders. Hopefully, this effort will mark the beginning of a sustained push for more responsible trustee oversight of athletics.

In short, gone are the days when a board member's primary responsibility relating to athletics was boosterism and attending games. There is, however, a fine line between a board's responsibility to establish and articulate institutional vision and direction and its becoming overly involved in day-to-day athletics department decision making. College athletics' history is littered with examples of the adverse effect of overzealous alumni and board members, the prime example being the direct involvement of boards in hiring a football or basketball coach when they do not perform the same function for academic departments. While it can be difficult striking such a balance, if presidential action is to be effective, it must have the backing of the board of trustees. To this end, trustees must explicitly endorse presidential authority in all matters of athletics governance, making it clearly understood that presidents bear the burden of leadership for the conduct of the institution, both in the classrooms and on the playing fields.

Simple logic suggests that as presidents become more engaged in athletics issues, so too will boards. But far more significant is that the nature of board involvement will change dramatically. Not only are board agenda items relating to athletics sure to increase, due to the emotionally charged atmosphere that envelopes athletics programs, but these issues will be significantly more controversial and far more difficult for boards to navigate.

For example, not only will trustees be looked upon to play a crucial role in determining the type of athletics program that will best serve the college or university, but they will be forced to consider the most fundamental issue relating to the role of athletics in higher education: whether the institution, in its efforts to fulfill its public mission, is best served by sponsoring athletics as currently structured. Once decisions regarding these issues have been made, it will be imperative that board members and other institutional leaders publicly and aggressively support these actions.

Given their responsibility to serve as the nexus between the public and the institution, trustees' perspective regarding athletics must become broader and further reaching. While some may consider this increased expectation a stretch, it is justified. There are significant problems within our nation's system of organized sport that trustees and presidents are being asked to provide leadership in addressing. As they step to the plate of athletics reform, it is crucial that trustees do so with the realization that the priorities they demonstrate in addressing the issue will have an impact that resonates far beyond their campus.

Boards must ask the following questions regarding the role that college athletics plays in our culture: Is higher education's role in sponsoring elite athletics, a relationship that has far too often resulted in the sacrificing of academic integrity at the alter of athletic glory, endangering America's educational and economic welfare by promoting values and encouraging behavior that runs counter to sound educational principles? By embracing the principles and behaviors of the professional sports system, has higher education become less able to meet its responsibility to provide the leadership necessary to enable our country to meet the intellectual challenges of the new millennium? While this assessment of college athletics' cultural impact may seem overblown, given their role as the nexus between the institution and our society, these are clearly issues trustees must consider.

Furthermore, trustees must thoughtfully consider whether our nation's long-term health interests are best served by higher education's sponsorship of the current professional sports model, a model that is being emulated by our high schools. As mentioned in chapter 2, the distortion of the value and purpose of sport in our culture has lead to the evolution of a sports system that is badly out of step with our nation's health needs. Boards must thoughtfully consider whether our education and public health needs are better served by adopting a system based on the European club-sport model.

While boards are being challenged to meet their responsibilities as the nexus between the public and the institution, they face a difficult conundrum. At a time when intercollegiate athletics appears to be more popular than ever, should institutions continue to sponsor intercollegiate athletics programs as currently structured, despite the fact that most of the rationales upon which these programs are based have been exposed as myths? And with increasing evidence that the impact of elite athletics on our schools and communities is becoming more negative, what is higher education's role in providing leadership to address that negative impact?

In meeting these evolving responsibilities, trustees will require a framework within which they can make reasoned decisions regarding athletics. For example, any meaningful discussion regarding the future role of athletics on campus must begin with a clear understanding of its core functions, values, and purposes. Boards must be clear as to what is expected of athletics departments regarding their contribution to institutional mission. Trustees must also be honest about whether the athletics department is fulfilling its purposes. If athletics departments are not delivering results for what are alleged to be their primary functions, what can be done to ensure that they do? And, if it is determined that athletics departments cannot meet these objectives, should such programs continue to be sponsored by the institution?

For over one hundred years, higher education leaders have established athletics policy based largely upon myths, half-truths, and anecdotal information. But with athletics being such a visible and influential campus entity, such decision-making strategies do not serve institutional purposes well. From the NCAA-mandated institutional self-study and certification program to a litany of studies from independent researchers on subjects ranging from finances to student-athlete academic performance, there is a steadily growing body of empirical data regarding athletics available to institutional decision makers. Not only must academic leaders address athletics issues directly, they must also insist on obtaining and utilizing solid empirical data to do so. This is particularly important when evaluating athletics' impact on institutional finances, educational values and priorities, campus culture, and public relations.

Finally, institutions of higher education must structure themselves according to what will enable them to effectively meet the most critical needs of the society they are meant to serve. If, for example, a particular department does not meet a clear need and no longer contributes to the central purpose of the institution in direct and vital ways, serious consideration should be given to restructuring, downsizing, or eliminating it. If athletics departments claim to be part of the educational institution, they ought to be subject to the same scrutiny and standards of accountability as other parts of the institution.

This leads to what may be the most important issue facing trustees regarding the role of athletics on their campuses. As articulated in the previous chapter, the role and impact of athletics on campus is, to a large degree, a product of institutional structure. When athletics departments are stand-alone enterprises, the propensity for them to undermine academic values and institutional mission is high. It does not take a management-policy expert to determine that integrating the athletics department into the administrative and governance structure of the university greatly enhances the ability to utilize athletics to contribute to institutional mission. Thus, trustees must seriously consider, as they did in the case of Vanderbilt University, a strategy to accomplish this structural change.

While change of this magnitude will be contentious, trustees are responsible for structuring the institution to meet its mission most effectively. Only until athletics departments become a part of, rather than apart from, institutional structure and academic culture, will athletics' full educational potential be realized. Once such change has been discussed and approved, trustees must fully support their president in implementing that change.

The challenge for trustees is to provide the leadership and exhibit the courage to honestly assess athletics' place on campus and to establish an athletics department incentive and measurement system designed to more effectively harness athletics' tremendous potential to contribute more directly to institutional mission and to the broader purposes of higher education.

PRESIDENTIAL RESPONSIBILITY: RESTRUCTURING THE INSTITUTION AND EMPOWERING OTHERS

The most important and successful development in the history of college athletics reform is how presidents, over the last two decades, have systematically consolidated and exerted their influence through the establishment of a structure and governance system through which they can formally implement and enact principles and programs relating to reform. The result is that there is no longer any doubt that presidents not only should be in charge but are, in fact, in charge. Through much hard work and persistence, presidents have empowered themselves to a degree where they can structure college athletics to represent whatever they want.

Despite this success, it is debatable whether college athletics, from an operational standpoint, is much better off than it was in 1982. Despite the fanfare that accompanied various academic reforms, presidents' actual impact has been less than revolutionary. As evidenced by the steady stream of scandals of 2003 and 2004, the professional model, with all that it represents and requires, remains intact. As a result, it continues to undermine the integrity of our educational system.

While recent reforms have been successful in that the structure to enable reform, centered on presidential authority, has been successfully established, the substance of reform—raising academic standards—has largely failed. In other words, while successfully empowering themselves to assume their rightful responsibility to govern and initiate change, presidents have been far less successful in choosing which aspects of the enterprise to use that influence to reform. Thus, it is time for presidents to focus their energies and influence on the aspect of the athletics enterprise that will truly lead to meaningful, systemic, long-lasting change: dismantling the professional model by eliminating athletic scholarships.

Addressing these broader concerns through the elimination of the athletic scholarship at the national level and institutional restructuring at the campus level will not be easy. It will test the courage and resolve of presidents as never before. Scholarships are the "third rail" of college athletics reform because the issue is so closely tied to race. Eliminating athletic scholarships will create an uproar and public outcry regarding "lost educational opportunities," particularly for black athletes. But if presidents want to reform athletics in a meaningful way, they must be willing to fight through what will be significant resistance and public outcry.

Due to the "radioactive" nature of this issue, presidents must acknowledge that they will not be able to carry through this effort without significant support from other groups with a stake in American higher education. That being the case, presidents must embark on an effort to further develop the critical mass necessary to support them when they take on this contentious issue. Specifically, they must shift their energies from empowering themselves to leading and empowering other key reform groups: boards, faculty, coaches, athletics administrators, and athletes.

To this end, presidents must clearly articulate why these groups have a stake in reform, what their responsibilities are in the reform effort, how they can meet these responsibilities, and, finally, to challenge them to do so. While presidents have been more aggressive in challenging boards to be more responsible in exercising their oversight responsibilities, empowering faculty, athletics administrators, and coaches may be more difficult. Faculty have always struggled with presidents over issues of institutional governance, including finances, curriculum, and institutional vision. In the area of athletics reform, however, presidents must articulate the fact that the interests of presidents and faculty are aligned. While there may be some differences as to the proper path, the goal is the same.

Building trust with the coaching and athletics communities may prove more challenging. One unintended consequence of the presidents' success in establishing themselves as being the key drivers of reform is that it has resulted in some resentment and alienation on the part of athletics administrators and coaches. These groups have sometimes felt that they are on the receiving end of reform rather than having a common stake and role in the reform of college athletics.

That aside, everyone has a stake in and role in the reform effort. Presidents, as the undisputed leaders of the reform movement, may have the most at stake. Clearly, the public recognizes the hypocrisy that eats away at the core values of an educational institution that sponsors a professional sports operation. While fans may not want to eliminate the entertainment college sports provides, they understand that colleges and universities have sold a piece of their souls in the pursuit of athletic glory and the financial rewards that accompany it. As a result, higher education's public credibility has suffered. If presidents do not display the will, courage, and wisdom necessary to systemically reform what is the most highly visible component of the higher education enterprise, how will they be able to muster the credibility necessary to provide effective leadership on the many other critical social and educational challenges facing our country?

To meet these challenges, presidents must articulate, not only to campus constituents but also the public, why reform is important, identify their roles and responsibilities, and challenge and empower members of these groups to meet these responsibilities. While they must lead the reform effort, presidents will not be able to achieve true reform until they have the necessary critical mass of trustees, faculty, coaches, athletics administrators, and athletes to support the extremely difficult decisions they must make and direction they must take the reform movement. Their challenge is to continue to build the growing critical mass and inspire it to coalesce in a way that will result in the meaningful change that is clearly in the best interest not only of American higher education but also our society generally.

FACULTY: GET INVOLVED!

Throughout the history of American higher education, faculty members have been most responsible for defining and defending institutional academic values. Because the professional model of athletics has come to undermine those values, faculty responsibility to become directly engaged in the issue is clear. The critical mass necessary to force substantive change simply cannot be achieved without significant faculty involvement, if for no other reason than their sheer size as a higher education constituency. Thus, the faculty is well positioned to provide presidents and boards with the momentum and support necessary to transform reform concepts into substantive change.

Traditionally, it has been at this point where discussion regarding the role of faculty in athletics reform breaks down. The common perception regarding faculty is that they are concerned only with their narrow discipline and have little interest in athletics issues. Thus, to think or expect their meaningful, sustained involvement with the issue is a pipe dream. While true in the past, the landscape not only of American higher education but also our society as it relates to athletics has changed too dramatically to expect that faculty will remain disengaged from such an important issue. Faculty members are like anyone else. They are interested in and concerned with issues that affect their lives and livelihood. While what transpires in athletics has always impacted faculty to some degree, what has changed is that athletics' impact is not only increasing but it is becoming clearer that that impact is far more direct than previously imagined. We can no longer deny that college sports, particularly big-time college sports, have evolved to a point where they are in direct conflict with academic values and integrity. These are the very principles that faculty are most responsible for defending.

To inspire faculty to become a part of the growing critical mass for reform, they must be convinced that what transpires in athletics affects them in a very personal way. To commit the time, energy, and emotion necessary to contribute to efforts to integrate athletics into the mainstream academic community more effectively, faculty must recognize the very direct connection between athletics' impact and their fundamental professional responsibilities. This connection must be demonstrated not only at those big-time NCAA Division I institutions but *all* schools that sponsor intercollegiate athletics.

As cited in chapter 1, a growing body of research is making this connection much clearer. As long-held myths regarding athletics' supposed positive impact on fund-raising, campus culture, admissions, fiscal integrity, and academic performance are shattered, it is becoming increasingly clear that faculty members at virtually every school are influenced by what transpires in athletics departments in very direct ways.

Given this direct impact on academic values, curriculum, funding, and educational integrity, faculty's stake in reform is enormous. Therefore, faculty members must contribute to the growing critical mass for reform by becoming engaged in the issue at some level. If nothing else, faculty owe it to themselves and other faculty to become more knowledgeable regarding that impact. While this may sound simple, the fact is, it has been faculty indifference that has been a major contributing factor in athletics' unchecked growth and influence.

At the same time, faculty must make the effort to create an environment conducive to their input. Many faculty consider athletics higher education's "evil empire." But rather than continuing to degrade athletics from the safety of their ivory towers, faculty members must acknowledge the fact that athletics not only are here to stay (although not necessarily in their present form) but, if managed properly, have tremendous potential to contribute to institutional mission. Despite their flaws, sports can be an effective educational tool, and their potential as a socialization tool can complement academic curricula. The resources inherent in big-time athletics programs—admired coaches and student-athletes—present opportunities for athletics to contribute to higher education's mission. Few other programs on campus have such potential to serve as a unifying element for the university. And one needs only to take note of the tens of thousands of people who attend games on campuses and the millions who watch them on television to recognize athletics' unique potential to contribute to institutional mission with its tremendous visibility and influence. To dismiss athletics as trivial is to waste it. Thus, the challenge for faculty is to influence the goals and structure of athletics programs in ways that harness their tremendous potential to contribute more effectively to the goals and mission of the institution while limiting their propensity to undermine academic values.

The most fundamental role of faculty is to safeguard the integrity of the classroom and the student's educational process and progress. In the case of athletics, this influence must also take the shape of safeguarding the academic experience of athletes and managing athletics' impact on campus culture. Fortunately, over the last two decades, the slow march to build critical mass for reform has created more vehicles through which faculty can exert influence over the values and conduct of the athletics department. As a result, opportunities for faculty to contribute to the growing critical mass for reform have never been greater.

Historically, faculty involvement in reform has been limited to the random faculty member speaking out on campus or fighting against meaningless courses or degrees designed to keep athletes eligible. In most cases, these professors were isolated, ostracized, and harassed, their voices shouted down by the athletics establishment and their fate sealed by faculty indifference. Against such odds, it is no wonder that most faculty members lost interest in fighting the system.

There are now, however, several much safer and more productive ways for faculty members to become engaged in athletics reform. At the campus level, most institutions have a faculty committee charged with reviewing athletics department policies on academics, scheduling, and goals. The NCAA's required certification review offers another opportunity to have an impact on the direction of the athletics department.

Another potential opportunity for faculty to become more actively engaged is through involvement in institutional student-athlete committees. In an effort to provide athletes with more input into the athletics department decision-making process, institutions are required to form student-athlete advisory committees. Faculty should have a liaison representative on such committees and should be kept abreast of the committee's actions and recommendations.

Finally, the NCAA requires that institutions have a formalized exit-interview program for athletes. This presents an excellent opportunity for faculty to become more informed about the student-athlete experience. At the very least, the results of such interviews should be communicated to the faculty. Athletics committees, the NCAA certification program, the student-athlete advisory committee, and the exit-interview program present opportunities for faculty to learn more about and influence the direction of their institution's athletics programs.

Perhaps the best way for faculty to exert influence regarding athletics at the campus level is through the faculty senate. Traditionally, faculty senates have given only cursory attention to athletics matters. As athletics have come to have a larger and more significant impact on institutional culture and mission, faculty senates must develop athletics as a higher priority item. There is ample evidence to suggest that faculty senates are gearing up to do so. For example, the faculty senates at eight Pacific-10 Conference schools passed resolutions in 2003 calling for their presidents to begin discussing ways to curb the "arms race" and commercialization in college sports. This was followed by similar resolutions at many Big 10 Conference schools and several other Division I-A institutions and has since evolved into the Coalition on Intercollegiate Athletics (COIA), an alliance of more than forty Division I faculty senates that has pledged support for the reform movement in intercollegiate athletics.

Working through faculty senates to achieve critical mass may be the most promising and powerful tool for faculty involvement. While it may be unreasonable to expect an overwhelmingly large percentage of faculty members to become actively engaged in athletics reform, faculty senate members, by virtue of their involvement in the senate, have accepted the responsibility of faculty leadership. Central to these leadership responsibilities is a role in defining academic and institutional values, including those that are impacted by athletics.

There are also an increasing number of opportunities to become involved at the conference and national levels. In addition to the long-standing opportunities through conference, NCAA, and AAUP committees, over the past few years, other faculty organizations have emerged and begun to play a role in building critical mass for reform. As mentioned in chapters 5 and 6, the creation of the Drake Group in 2000, COIA in 2002, and the National Institute for Sports Reform in 2003 offer faculty the opportunity to become involved in reform on the national level. These organizations demonstrate another important requirement for building critical mass; the ability for various individuals and groups to build coalitions around common issues of concern. While the Drake Group and COIA are focusing primarily on issues of academic integrity, involvement in the conference or NCAA structure can provide opportunities to address important governance issues. In short, there are many issues, angles, and aspects of athletics reform, with various emerging groups and structures coalescing around these issues. The result is that there are now more opportunities for a faculty member to do his or her part in the athletics reform movement.

Increased faculty knowledge of and involvement with athletics is laudable and welcome. However, faculty must also understand that there is more to increased involvement in the governance of athletics than simply pointing fingers and criticizing athletics as being out of control. With increased involvement comes increased responsibility. Thus, faculty members would do well to ask themselves, What if our athletics administrators and coaches meet the new standards relating to athletics reform? What if the football coach recruits better students, does more to help them graduate, runs a clean program, and becomes more involved in the university community, but fields a 7-4 team rather than the expected 9-2? In such cases, there may be intense pressure from alumni, boosters, and the media to fire that coach. Will faculty back the coach who has met these new expectations? Will faculty stand firm for academic and institutional integrity when athletics reform reaches this critical juncture on their campus? Increased faculty involvement comes with a price tag that at times may be heavy—but it is one that faculty must be willing to pay.

There is also some risk to faculty in meeting their responsibility as guardians of academic standards and the quality of the students' experience. The faculty is responsible for ensuring that courses and majors are legitimate. Myles Brand said, as reported in a February 14, 2005, column in the *NCAA News*, "Faculty members own the curriculum—they have oversight of the courses and majors, and they have the authority to cull out those that do not meet the rigors of the institutional mission" (Brand, 2005a, p. A-4). While faculty responsibility in this area has always been clear, the question is whether they will be willing to pay the price to fully exercise this authority as it relates to athletes.

While some faculty members will continue to believe that athletics is something they do not have the time to learn about, the fact is, athletics impacts faculty and institutional mission in a wide variety of ways. Thus, it is imperative for faculty, as guardians of academic integrity and the students' academic experience, to take advantage of these opportunities to become more engaged with this important campus activity.

There are other areas in which faculty can play a role in reform. For over a hundred years, campus leaders have based athletics policies largely on myths, anecdotes, and propaganda from coaches, athletics administrators, sports-crazed alumni, and star-struck media. This history provides faculty an excellent opportunity to assert their campus influence. As the primary guardians of academic integrity, faculty must advance the dialogue regarding the appropriate role of athletics on campus and ensure that such discussions and subsequent decisions are based on facts. To this end, faculty can have a major impact on reform efforts by doing what faculty do: research. Areas of study should include athletics' impact on finances, campus culture, admissions, minority recruitment, allocation of scholarship dollars, public relations, institutional imaging, alumni relations, and institutional values and priorities. In short, faculty must assume a central leadership position as we search for the truth about the influence of sports on higher education.

Finally, faculty can play a critical role in an area relating to reform that has received little attention: curriculum development. There are two areas in which faculty must provide leadership in this regard. As will be outlined later in this chapter, the biggest challenge facing the coaching community is rebuilding the "coach-as-educator" model. This will require a significant educational effort, from developing challenging coaching curricula to be offered by graduate schools to continuing-education programs to keep coaches current in the field to new coaching orientation programs at the conference and institutional levels. Faculty can also play a critical role in developing, testing, and conducting such programs. Simply put, it will not be sufficient for faculty to simply challenge coaches to become more integrated into the academic community. They must also develop and present the educational programs that will train future coaches and athletics administrators to meet the challenges that a more educationally centered athletics program would present.

The second curriculum-based issue faculty must address relates to public health. Under our current system, the responsibility to develop elite teams and athletes rests with our educational institutions. From a public health standpoint, this emphasis must shift to the point where the primary function of our educational system is to emphasize broad-based participation in activities that can be practiced for a lifetime. If our educational system is to successfully meet the long-term physical fitness needs of our increasingly obese populace, school-based physical education curricula must be revamped. To do so, universities must rethink how future physical education teachers are trained and physical education curricula are developed. This will require a dramatic change in the preparation of the physical education teachers of the future. Again, faculty must take a lead in this transformation.

In the end, faculty can no longer afford to dismiss athletics and its institutional impact and their responsibility to become more engaged with athletics reform. Because athletics will always be a part of higher education, it will continue to have a very direct impact on faculty and their institutions. Thus, it is clearly in faculty members' interest to become more active in exerting their influence to shape that impact. Most important, however, is that continued neglect in this area will have a significant effect on faculty's most important responsibility as the primary guardians of academic integrity and the students' educational experience. This core faculty responsibility applies to all students, including athletes. If the faculty neglects its responsibility for the academic and personal welfare of athletes, they run the risk of becoming academically and institutionally irrelevant. Refusing to address the academic exploitation of even one group of students will ultimately be seen as an abdication of their responsibility in this area for all students.

REBUILDING THE COACH-AS-EDUCATOR MODEL

Many within higher education see coaches as the prime example of the excesses of intercollegiate athletics: being overpaid, having oversized egos, and being more interested in securing their next shoe contract than the academic and personal welfare of their athletes. Coaches believe these accusations are unjustified, claiming they have simply responded to expectations and a reward system that has changed over the past few decades. According to coaches, the message they receive from presidents, boards, athletics directors, fans, the media, and alumni is that winning, generating revenue, and providing entertainment are more important than education. As a result, they have modified their behavior to meet these expectations. For the most part, they are right. How many winning coaches are fired for low graduation rates? This is why coaches resent being cast as the poster children for reform. This resentment has led to coaches being viewed as a very visible, vocal, and powerful force against reform.

Regardless of these perceptions and this history, coaches remain the most influential people in the lives of athletes, as well as highly visible university employees. Thus, it is imperative that they play a major role in reform. That said, coaches must recognize that this history will prevent them from having much of a direct influence over the general reform process. Their role and place in the reform efforts being conducted by presidents, boards, and faculty will be limited. This does not mean, however, that coaches can not be major players in the reform movement. Rather than trying to influence the general reform environment, their focus should be internal. Specifically, the coaching community must concentrate on reforming the coaching profession by rebuilding the "coach-as-educator" model. In short, the coaching profession must get back to its educational roots.

Historically, the primary justification for coaches being a part of the educational community has centered on the idea that coaches are teachers and educators. A coach's classroom, it is said, is the field or court where the lessons—discipline, sportsmanship, and teamwork—are as important as those learned in the chemistry lab or debate club. Yet, many within academe and among the general population have come to question whether coaches contribute to the academic community in meaningful ways and whether they are, as they claim, teachers and educators. On far too many campuses, coaches are viewed as entertainers and entrepreneurs concerned more with winning games than educating athletes. In short, the coach-as-educator model has gone the way of the leather football helmet and the two-handed set shot. Deserved or not, this alienation from their traditional, core purpose continues to hamper efforts to rebuild the integrity of college athletics. It is in this area where coaches can have a major impact on reform.

What can the coaching community do to help restore the coach-as-educator ideal? To appreciate the answer, it is important to understand the recent evolution of the coaching profession.

Twenty-five years ago, the most important hiring criteria for a college assistant coach were teaching ability and head coaching experience. These individuals were usually found at the high school level—head coaches with master's degrees and years of classroom teaching experience. Typically, such candidates coached because they loved young people, believed in the value of education, and viewed sports as another vehicle for teaching. Today, the most important credential for an assistant coach is the personality of a slick-looking, fast-talking salesman who can sell the program to high school All-Americans. The qualities and background of a committed educator are simply no longer valued components of an assistant coach's credentials. Because college coaching now offers opportunities to earn significant amounts of money, to appear on national television, and to become a media darling, it can be argued that the motivation for young people entering the profession has changed as well. The combination of these changing expectations, credentials, and motivations has created professional coaches in the collegiate atmosphere. As evidence of this change, consider the increasingly common practice, particularly in the sport of football, of coaches moving from the professional ranks to the college programs and vice versa. If college athletics in general and coaches in particular are to be accepted as valuable, contributing members of the higher education community, the coaching community must begin to address the deterioration of the coach-as-educator model.

Coaching is a teaching profession, with its most important priority being not necessarily teaching the game but, rather, using the game to teach about the importance of staying in school, investing in education, and life itself. But the title of "coach" rings hollow when the only criteria necessary to be called one is being able to hang a whistle around your neck. While there is no standard route to becoming a college coach, it is becoming increasingly likely for young coaches to move directly from a playing career to an assistant coaching position, rather than first earning a master's degree, followed by teaching and coaching at the high school level.

For example, according to a 2004 study conducted by the National Institute for Sports Reform, only 29.9 percent of Division I men's basketball coaches and 33.5 percent of Division I women's basketball coaches possess a master's degree. (Gerdy, Staurowsky, and Svare, 2004). This study illustrates the need for coaches to demonstrate their commitment to education by investing more heavily in the educational process. Coaches must embrace the fact that the correlation between educational background and one's credibility as a teacher, and thus influence and effectiveness in promoting education and character, is very direct. Expecting that a college coach possess a master's degree is an important and reasonable standard.

If coaches are to rebuild their credibility as educators, their level of degree attainment becomes important. In the academic community, educational attainment is respected and carries influence; it is the currency of the higher education community. Whether such an attitude is right or wrong is not the issue. What is significant is that athletics departments must function within this environment.

Although earning an advanced degree is not absolutely essential to being an effective teacher, investing the time, expense, and effort to earn such a degree demonstrates an individual's belief in, and commitment to, the value of education. Generally, coaches who have earned advanced degrees should be more effective teachers and educational role models because they have demonstrated a commitment to, and made a personal investment in, the educational process. Teaching is a profession; one that requires commitment, dedication, and preparation. Coaches must be willing to increase the standards and expectations necessary to be considered professionals.

Furthermore, once hired, coaches must be provided with meaningful opportunities to refine and develop their teaching skills. Most professional development opportunities offered through coaching associations focus on coaching techniques and strategies directly related to the game. But in order for coaches to be effective teachers, the NCAA, conferences, and, in particular, coaches' associations must provide them with opportunities to develop and refine their teaching skills. Many professions, including the medical and legal professions, require in-service training on a regular basis.

Highlighting the academic backgrounds of coaches also presents an excellent opportunity for coaches to partner with faculty members in developing and implementing appropriate master's level curricula for the coaching profession. Such curricula should include components relating to student development, the role of higher education in America, the role of athletics within higher education, media relations, and the responsibilities inherent in being a highly visible representative of a university. There is a lot more to coaching than game strategy and recruiting, and it is imperative to instill in future coaches an understanding of the role and responsibilities of being an educator on a college campus.

In short, the most significant thing that coaches can do to carve out a meaningful role for themselves in the reform movement is to look at their own profession and begin to strengthen it by working to reconnect it to the educational process and community. To do so will require a significant effort to reestablish the coach-as-educator model by concentrating on the educational and professional development of coaches.

While efforts to restore the coach-as-educator model should be the cornerstone of the coaching community's reform agenda, there is another important function that coaches must perform: advocacy. Specifically, coaches must use their visibility to drive a national dialogue regarding evaluation criteria for coaches within an educational institution. Any effort to change coaching behavior or to strengthen a coach's link to the educational community will be fruitless unless the criteria upon which coaching success is determined is clear. For too long, presidents, boards, and the media have called for coaches to be more responsible educators, on one hand, while judging them solely on wins and losses, on the other. The fact is, there must be more to evaluating the success of a college coach than his or her win/loss record.

For example, where a football coach has been expected to maintain a 10-1 record and receive a major bowl bid every year, the university community must begin to adjust those expectations to accept an 8-3 or 7-4 record and a bowl bid, particularly if the coach runs a clean program that produces quality, well-rounded individuals who graduate, are positive role models, and contribute to society after their playing days are over. In short, it is time to begin to hold presidents and board members to their stated high ideals. To do so, coaches must use their visibility to initiate a national dialogue regarding the expectations, qualifications, and evaluation criteria for a coach at an educational institution.

Furthermore, coaches' associations should aggressively call for a reexamination of coaches' contracts. Specifically, such contracts should be restructured to include financial incentives for coaches to continue to invest in the educational process and advance their degrees. Is there a single coach's contract that includes a financial bonus to encourage a coach with a bachelor's degree to earn a master's, or a coach with a master's to earn a PhD? Placing a greater emphasis on a coach's level of education is a way to provide more substance to the argument that coaches are teachers and educators.

While it is easy to criticize coaches for losing sight of their core purpose as educators, presidents, faculty, board members, and the media have also been responsible for the erosion of the coach-as-educator model. Thus, every constituency within the educational community has a stake in helping coaches reconnect to that core purpose. Only until coaches are, once again, respected and contributing members of the educational community will true reform be realized. But it is the coaching community itself that must initiate this process. It is imperative for coaches to do this, as the very future of their profession—a noble, teaching profession—is at risk.

But simply recommitting to the philosophical underpinnings of coaching as a teaching profession will not be enough to restore coaches' credibility as educators. This philosophical commitment must be accompanied by specific actions designed to show that coaches are indeed committed to being responsible and credible reform partners.

For example, coaches could take a bold step toward restoring their educational credibility by advocating the elimination of off-campus recruiting. In today's world of videotape and independent scouting services, off-campus recruiting is no longer necessary. More important, however, is that the tremendous amount of time and resources devoted to recruiting has come to overshadow the coach's primary role as an educator. Eliminating off-campus recruiting would allow coaches to spend more time teaching and mentoring their current student-athletes. It would also provide more opportunity to participate in the professional development or graduate school programs identified earlier. With the elimination of off-campus recruiting, the importance of hiring assistant coaches with strong academic, mentoring, and coaching skills, as opposed to recruiting skills, will increase. And without the burden of recruiting travel, many quality high school coaches, particularly veteran coaches with families who have had no interest in becoming college coaches, may now consider such opportunities. This change will also provide more opportunities for coaches to become integrated into the mainstream campus community.

Just as the increased emphasis on recruiting resulted in a shift in the desired qualifications of assistant coaches from those of an educator to those of a salesperson, eliminating off-campus recruiting would have the effect of reversing this trend. Certainly there is the chance that this change would result in coaches making a few more recruiting mistakes. But the cost savings in these days of the athletics "arms race," its effect on the desired academic and professional profile of coaches, the increased involvement in mentoring enrolled student-athletes, and the chance to become more involved in the campus community far outweigh those few "mistakes."

While some may consider the above-mentioned change radical, the fact is, the coaching profession and all that it represents is being seriously challenged. That being the case, nothing short of bold, innovative, profession-changing action is required. At issue is whether there comes a point at which coaches have ventured so far from their roots as educators that their justification for being on campus collapses. Is it possible for coaches to become so divorced from their core purpose that they lose all credibility as teachers? It is in this way that the very soul of the coaching profession is at stake.

The renewed push for college athletics reform presents tremendous challenges, opportunities, and, ultimately, very stark choices for coaches. The central theme of this shift is the need to clearly distinguish between what coaches *do*, which is play games, and what they must be *about*, which is education. In other words, which coaching model do coaches believe in and wish to perpetuate: the coach as educator or the coach as the head of a professional sports franchise? And, is the coach-as-educator model an important enough principle to use their considerable influence and visibility to fight for?

The educationally empowered student-athletes that the elimination of athletic scholarships would produce would undoubtedly present significant challenges for coaches. Because they would not have nearly as much influence and control over the student-athlete, coaches would have to adjust their coaching styles accordingly. But if coaches are true to what they claim to be about, they should embrace such challenges. Coaches claim to be educators who use athletics as a vehicle for supplementing the educational process. Although winning is important, coaching is, first and foremost, about education. If that is not the case, then coaches have no business being on a college campus.

With recurring revelations of their involvement in academic fraud and illegal benefits scandals, coaches have come to be seen as being a major part of the problem in athletics. This is unfortunate because many coaches believe in and act according to the coach-as-educator model. That said, there is no denying that while they are not entirely to blame for sports' win-at-all-costs culture, coaches have undoubtedly been major contributors to its evolution.

While most will protest the elimination of athletic scholarships, this change may actually provide coaches with an opportunity to scale back those win-at-all-costs expectations and to reaffirm the educational component of their job descriptions. If coaches truly believe they are educators rather than entertainers, educational role models rather than entrepreneurial profit centers, they would welcome a change that would shift the student-athlete/coach relationship from one that is driven by professional principles to one that affords the opportunity to forge a relationship with their student-athletes that is driven by educational principles and goals.

Although there will always be pressure to win, this change would reduce those expectations because the fundamental relationship between the coach and the athlete would shift from one that is based almost entirely on athletic performance to one that has a clear educational dimension that coaches would be forced to respect and appreciate. A shift toward an educationally centered model of college sports would also result in a corresponding shift toward a more educationally motivated model of coaching. Thus, eliminating the athletic scholarship presents a tremendous opportunity for the coaching community—an opportunity to reestablish the coach as educator as a legitimate and credible model.

In short, it is "crunch time" for coaches. Successfully navigating the current landscape of reform will require strong leadership to take the hard steps necessary to rebuild the profession's credibility. The landscape for reform is ripe with opportunity for those who want to make a difference by contributing to the growing critical mass for reform. There is no reason why coaches should not be an integral part of that critical mass.

ATHLETICS ADMINISTRATORS: LOWERING THE INTENSITY

Other than the president or chancellor, there is no more difficult university job than athletics director. The most difficult of these jobs are at the NCAA Division I level, where athletics directors face a very difficult balancing act, constantly placating various constituencies. Faculty demand academic accountability, academic administrators demand fiscal responsibility, media demand transparency, athletes demand attention, coaches demand resources and emotional support, the NCAA demands rules compliance, television executives and corporate sponsors demand access, alumni and fans demand wins, and citizens of a state demand part ownership of their state university's team.

While managing the interests of these diverse constituencies, athletics directors must also balance the budget in an increasingly demanding and competitive economic climate. This, of course, requires winning teams. If that is not stressful enough, athletics directors go to bed every night dreading that phone call informing them of an athlete's brush with the law or a morning headline breaking the news of an NCAA rules violation. Perhaps most wearing is the constant tension that goes with heading a program that is viewed by many as being rife with hypocrisy.

Thus, of any constituency in the higher education community, athletics directors may reap the most benefit from the changes advocated in this book. The elimination of the athletic scholarship and the dismantling of the professional sports model of college athletics would greatly benefit athletics administrators because these measures would, in Myles Brands's words, "turn down the volume of athletics" by significantly reducing the tension, intensity, and hypocrisy of everything associated with major college athletics.

Most significant, perhaps, is that, by dismantling the professional model, athletics administrators will no longer be placed in the uncomfortable position of having to sell a program on educational grounds when it is plain for all to see that what they are running is a professional sports and entertainment franchise. De-professionalizing the enterprise will ease this tension by realigning sales rhetoric with the actual product. Further, with the structural changes advocated in chapter 6, the pressure to balance budgets and maintain a self-sustaining enterprise would diminish significantly because the budget would be determined, allocated, and subsidized like all other university departments.

While some athletics administrators may resist surrendering a measure of their autonomy in managing athletics, if they truly believe that athletics supplements educational mission and that participation contributes to the personal development of young people, they should welcome such change. Similar to coaches, athletics administrators, through no great fault of their own, have lost sight of their purpose within the academic community, and, as a result, the management of athletics departments has suffered. If institutions are to maximize athletics' tremendous potential for contributing to institutional mission in timely and meaningful ways, athletics administrators must embrace the de-professionalization of the enterprise.

In short, it is in athletics administrators' best interests that such changes be realized because they would make their lives much less intense, pressure-packed, and "over the top." That being the case, athletics administrators must become willing and aggressive participants in the growing critical mass of those who are committed to meaningful, long lasting, progressive reform.

A BETTER DEAL FOR ALL ATHLETES

Eliminating the athletic scholarship is clearly in the best long-term interests of the athlete. As explained in chapter 6, such a change fundamentally rewrites the contract from being an agreement between the athlete and the coach based entirely on athletic performance to one between the student and the institution that remains in effect regardless of athletic performance. This shift empowers the athlete by providing a legitimate opportunity to be fully integrated into the student body and larger academic community.

Athletes are constantly forced to make decisions that pit their academic or social interests against their athletic interests. In the current system, with the threat of the elimination of their athletic scholarships hanging over their heads, invariably, athletes have to make decisions in favor of athletic interests. Because of the intense pressure to constantly show one's "commitment to the program," athletes are continually forced to make decisions that would further their athletic goals, while pushing their academic or social aspirations into the background. Like the muscle that atrophies from inactivity, the result is a dwindling of athletes' social and academic interests in favor of athletic interests. Although much in athletics, such as travel to new and exciting places, can expand the athlete's worldview, the result is that far too often the control that the athletic scholarship affords the coach results in narrowing the athlete's worldview and educational experience.

For example, if an athlete wants to go to a movie with a nonathlete but the coach has planned a social event with a booster of the program, the athlete feels pressure to attend the team function. Or, if a coach thinks a particular course or major will be too demanding and would thus affect athletic performance, it is "suggested" that the athlete enroll in one that will be less so. A student who wants to participate in athletics should not have to decide whether he should risk falling into disfavor with his or her coach over taking an afternoon class that interferes with practice time. And the stakes for falling into disfavor are high. Contrary to what many people believe, the athletic scholarship is not a four-year award but rather a one-year contract renewable at the discretion of the coach. For the student in a de-professionalized system, the institutional need-based financial aid agreement would allow educational priorities to prevail.

The fact is, the athletic scholarship creates significant barriers to all athletes in achieving what they want from the college athletics experience. Despite the impression one might get from reading the newspapers, the vast majority of participants in college sports strive for a genuine amateur, "student-athlete experience." For these individuals, the athletic scholarship places them in a "professional" operation. The excessive athletic demands required in such an operation prevent them from achieving their academic and personal goals. Why should there be any obstacles for a youngster, athlete or nonathlete, who wants to become more fully integrated into the student body and academic community? It is simply unconscionable for an educational institution to sponsor any activity that requires an exorbitant commitment of time and energy from participants resulting in their being unable to fully realize their academic goals. Thus, for the vast majority of athletes, elimination of the athletic scholarship is an infinitely better deal because it will better prepare them for the next fifty years of their lives by removing what have become significant barriers to academic achievement and a well-balanced educational experience.

Perhaps the best evidence of the potential impact of such a change is the fact that it would legitimize what has come to be the most glaring symbol of the hypocrisy of the current system. Eliminating the athletic scholarship and the professional model of intercollegiate athletics and thus educationally empowering the athlete would legitimize the term "student-athlete." Under such a system, a young person could truly achieve that noble distinction because coaches would not be able to dictate every aspect of the student-athlete's life.

Ironically, the athletic scholarship presents significant obstacles for elite athletes as well. If professional sports are a legitimate profession, why should those who have little interest in academics and want only to pursue a professional sports career be denied the best opportunity to maximize their potential to do so? If this is what they want to do, why should they be forced to participate in the charade of their college experience being "balanced" as required by the NCAA? Why should they have to masquerade as "student-athletes" when all they want to do is play ball? For these athletes, the best way to achieve that goal is not through the NCAA system, with its academic requirements and tight restrictions on practices and games, but rather through a sports-club system based on the European model.

The NCAA transfer rule provides an excellent example of how the NCAA system actually works against the elite athlete. If an athlete wants to transfer schools, he or she is required to sit out from competition for one year. Further, there are many out-of-season practice restrictions designed to safeguard the athlete's academic welfare. Are such rules really safeguards if the athlete has no interest in an academic experience? The fact is, the NCAA system does not permit the unfettered athletic development of elite athletes. For the elite athlete, the club system is a much better option.

Those who claim elite athletes would have nowhere to go to hone their skills, fail to appreciate how important it is to professional leagues to have a system to develop talent. Because our colleges and universities provide a developmental system for them, professional leagues have no incentive to develop minor leagues of their own. Once higher education stops catering to elite athletes with no interest in education, the professional leagues would create opportunities for those athletes to develop their skills. Elite athletes who are truly interested in education and earning a well-balanced college experience can continue to go to college on need-based financial aid and commit themselves to developing both academically and athletically. If at some point they are good enough to play professionally, the pros will sign them.

Let's be honest. The debate regarding seventeen- and eighteen-year-old athletes bypassing college to play professionally has always been more about race and money than about education. Why, for example, do college coaches and administrators think it is so important for basketball or football players to attend college immediately after high school but not tennis, golf, hockey, and baseball players? It is because basketball and football are revenue-generating sports for colleges while the other sports are not, and most elite athletes in the sports of football and basketball are black while those in the other sports are white. The fact is, attending college immediately after high school is not always in the best interests of elite athletes. As future baseball Hall of Fame pitcher Roger Clemons commented when his son Koby signed with the Houston Astros directly out of high school, "I think in professional baseball, he's going to get the instruction he needs" (Araton, 2005, p. C-19).

One of the great myths regarding intercollegiate athletics is that even elite athletes with no interest in participating in the academic process and being a part of the academic community are better off going to college. The fact is, it is not nearly as important *when* you earn a college degree as *whether* you earn it. These elite athletes can always enroll in college when their playing days are over. They can also stipulate in their professional contracts that the team will pay their future college tuition. Their educational experience would be more legitimate, worthwhile, and meaningful if they were to enroll when they are truly ready to learn and earn a degree.

Despite the initial perception that eliminating the athletic scholarship is not in the best interests of athletes, upon a closer and more honest examination, it becomes apparent that it is. This is because the current scholarship-driven model creates significant barriers for both the elite athlete and the individual who wants a well-balanced academic and athletic experience. Eliminating the athletic scholarship and dismantling the current professional model serves elite athletes more effectively, as they can pursue their athletic development without the barriers created by NCAA rules and academic standards. Those young people who wish to experience college as a true student-athlete will be better able to do so because the barriers to achieving that well-balanced academic, personal, and athletic experience that result from involvement in a professional sports operation will be removed.

SHAPING UP SCHOOL AND COMMUNITY SPORTS: DETERMINING THE TRUE COSTS

The major thrust of this book has been to call for a shift from the current school-based professional model to a community-based club system similar to the European model. Given its traditional role of providing leadership in addressing the broad cultural and societal issues of the day, the impetus for this change must come from higher education. This is why the prescriptive recommendations offered have focused on college athletics. This does not, however, mean that we should not begin to build the framework for carrying out these changes at the community, grade school, and high school levels.

As outlined in chapter 2, the current school-based model of organized sport is badly out of step with our nation's health needs. Specifically, our nation's system of organized sport has failed to promote the idea that sport for pure exercise is positive, fun, and healthy. Rather, athletics must be about winning and developing future all-stars and pros. This athletic elitism, beginning in youth sports leagues with the selection of all-star traveling teams of ten-year-olds, continues through high school and college. The result is that the best perform while all others watch.

Meanwhile, obesity in children has reached epidemic proportions in America.

One of the key fronts in the fight against this enormous health care issue is our grade schools, high schools, and community sports programs. Lifelong health and fitness habits are not developed by accident. They must be taught, nurtured, and practiced regularly from an early age. Our schools must play a role in this educational process by aggressively teaching and promoting the concept of fitness for life.

To this end, I called for a structural shift in the role of sports in our schools from the current, elite model, with its priorities of winning and developing future college and pro athletes, to one that would have as its fundamental purposes using athletics as a tool to supplement the educational development of participants and promoting broad-based participation in activities that can be practiced for a lifetime in the interests of public health. In this model, physical education requirements, intramural sports, and wellness programs would be expanded and improved, and the responsibility for the development of elite athletes and teams would shift from our schools to private sports clubs and professional teams.

Undoubtedly, cultural and community attitudes against moving elite athletics out of our high schools will be strong. Nevertheless, our schools must be structured according to what will best enable them to fulfill their responsibility to meet the educational and health needs of our children. While progressive change of this magnitude will not be easy or quick, to think that it will never occur is misguided. As we come to understand the significant societal costs associated with obesity, it is emerging as one of the most important public health issues of our time. Based on a comprehensive report recently issued by the National Academies' Institute of Medicine, schools and communities must play an important role in addressing the problem. The report correctly indicated that obesity should be attacked societally, not just individually.

Dr. Jeffrey Koplan, vice president for academic health affairs at Emory University and chairman of the committee that issued the report, acknowledged that we are at the early stages of what may be a decade-long process of changing public attitudes about the causes and cures for obesity: "What we found with other health matters—

fluoridation, bicycle helmets, smoking—is that you develop societal changes and then there is a shift in what is socially acceptable. It really isn't any different from banning smoking in restaurants. It required society as a whole to say, 'We don't want to see smoking in restaurants,' before legislation" (qtd. in "New Approach to Childhood Obesity Is Urged," 2004, p. A-20).

In other words, the type of change suggested in this book is, in fact, possible.

That begs the question, Where and how do we start?

Although not readily apparent, we are much further down the road to building the critical mass that drives community and cultural change than one might think. We are beginning to seriously discuss the issue on a consistent basis. Solutions like the one outlined here as well as many others are being developed, proposed, and debated. This represents a significant first step.

But moving from talk and proposals is a long and difficult path. It begins by developing and documenting the case for change in the educational system. This requires data. Ultimately, facts provide the basis for public understanding of the problem and the eventual drive toward change. For example, as data regarding the harmful effects of second-hand smoke accumulated, pressure began to mount for a ban in restaurants and workplaces. Cultural change occurs when the public understands that an impact extends beyond the individual to society generally. It is abundantly clear that the negative impact of obesity on public health care costs is enormous and growing.

Which brings us to the question of where to start in pushing for the changes necessary to better enable our schools to help our children in fighting this epidemic. Before a school board or a community can discuss, evaluate, and determine what role athletics should play at a school, it is critical that the true, direct costs of such programs be accurately determined and communicated. In determining these direct costs, two items must be considered.

First, because it is rare that athletics expenses appear as a specific line item in a school or district budget, it is difficult to obtain an accurate picture of the money and resources spent on sports. Transportation expenses for the football team, for example, are usually included in the transportation costs for the entire district. Insurance costs for athletics are usually meshed with the total insurance bill for the district. Maintenance fees for athletics facilities are generally rolled into the general budget. In most cases, these expenses are considered part of the "extracurricular activities" budget, which adds another layer through which to dig to determine exact athletics costs. Thus, school boards must look beyond the raw numbers to obtain an accurate financial accounting of the true cost of these programs.

Second, it is necessary to determine exactly how many athletes are served in these programs. For example, participation totals rarely recognize multiple sport participants. It is not uncommon for a school to boast of having 350 kids participating in school sports. But what looks like 350 students is often only 125 or 150 of the same kids each playing two or three sports.

Therefore, the first thing that community activists and school board members must accomplish is to obtain an accurate accounting of financial and participation numbers. Doing so would provide a better context against which to determine whether a school or a district is best utilizing scarce resources to serve all of its students and citizens and would serve as the foundation for discussion regarding the role that sports should play in our communities, grade schools, and high schools.

Another issue that school boards can address is the structure of the school day. As mentioned in chapter 2, if you were to structure the optimum academic learning environment for high school students, it would occur in the afternoon, without interruptions, and with a low teacher-to-student ratio. Currently, that environment exists, not for academic classes, but for after-school sports team practices. While budgetary restrictions will not usually permit a lower teacher-to-student ratio, certainly the school-day schedule could be modified to have sports practices in the morning and academic classes in the afternoon.

Meaningful, progressive reform of the magnitude advocated in this book will not be realized until the higher education community comes together to create the critical mass necessary to support such bold measures. While presidents can lead the charge, they can not push through change of the magnitude in these pages without the support of boards, faculty, coaches, athletics administrators, and athletes. In the final analysis, everyone has a meaningful role to play in the reform process. Everyone can and should contribute because we all have a stake in ensuring that our athletics departments contribute to the missions of our colleges and universities in timely, meaningful, and relevant ways.

COURAGE

There is really only one thing that requires real courage to say, and that is a truism.

—G. K. Chesterton

In the movie *Casablanca*, there is a scene where Louie, the chief of the local French police, is ordered by the commander of the occupying German army to shut down Rick's Café, a nightclub-casino frequented by French nationalists during World War II. Rick, played by Humphrey Bogart, protested. "On what grounds?" he asked. To which Louie replied, "I am shocked—shocked to discover there is gambling going on in here." No sooner had he spoken than a casino runner approached him, hand extended furtively, muttering, "Your winnings, sir."

While humorously depicting the hypocrisy of publicly stated ideals versus actual practice, the scene could very well be describing the behavior of higher education leaders regarding the role and impact of Division I athletics on our colleges and universities. Unfortunately, such behavior, which serves to erode higher education's integrity and credibility, is anything but funny.

Louie's feigned "shock" at the existence of a corrupt and unlawful activity in his favorite nightclub is played out on a regular basis by the media, higher education and athletics leaders, and the general public when it comes to the issue of the professional sports model of athletics on campus. Whether it is sex for recruits at the University of Colorado, academic fraud at the University of Georgia or St. Bonaventure University, the murder of a basketball player at Baylor University, or the abysmally low graduation rates of far too many March Madness basketball teams, the fact is, while we feign shock, we have come to accept such transgressions as the norm. Just as gambling in Rick's Café, though not openly acknowledged, was an accepted part of the nightclub's business, so too have corruption, hypocrisy, and scandal become a part of the business of professionalized college athletics.

The fact that such abuses no longer shock us is the most damning indictment of the current state of college sports, for it confirms that such corrupt practices can no longer be explained away as isolated incidents, a short-term crisis, or a situation-specific transgression. Rather, corruption and hypocrisy have become the very nature of the system. The abhorrent has become the norm. When such actions can no longer be denied or explained away it means that the system itself is the problem. Or, to cite another classic movie, "Pay no attention to that man behind the curtain." The Wizard of Oz has been revealed as a fraud.

FACING OUR FEARS

Change is difficult. Change, particularly the fundamental change advocated in these pages, can be frightening. Despite widespread agreement that athletics reform is necessary, fear of the unknown that such reform may bring causes us to settle for tinkering around the edges rather than pursuing bold, progressive reform. Any act of reform, no matter how modest, satisfies our need to feel that we are acting responsibly in addressing a flawed system while not assuming any significant risk. At the heart of our fear is the risk that aggressive reform will "kill the goose that lays the golden eggs." The problem, however, is that we know the goose itself is sick. While it is still laying eggs, those eggs are rotten. The evidence is becoming startlingly clear. It is not simply that professionalized college athletics has failed to meet most of the goals and purposes for which it was created. More damaging is the fact that the entire system is based on a lie. We claim it is about education when we know it is really about athletics and winning. We say it is "amateur" when we know it is built on the principles of the professional sports model.

Fear makes it difficult to gather the courage to pull the trigger on fundamental change. If we can not envision or imagine what change will eventually look like and lead to, we are inclined to stay with the familiar. Unless there is a measure of comfort with what fundamental change will result in, it will likely never occur. We fear what we cannot see or imagine. But, in the case of eliminating our departments of professional athletics, this fear is unfounded.

SAME AS IT EVER WAS

On one level, eliminating the departments of professional athletics by restructuring the scholarship agreement will profoundly change not only college athletics but also higher education and our society. Declaring that it is not appropriate for higher education to sponsor professional sports franchises and embracing an athletics model that is educationally centered will have an enormously positive impact on the credibility of presidents, trustees, faculty, and coaches. Demonstrating the courage and conviction to act decisively on this very visible issue will help restore the public's confidence in higher education as a vital American institution. With increased credibility and public trust come increased opportunities for higher education leaders to exert their leadership responsibilities in a more effective manner and, in the process, fulfill higher education's purpose more effectively.

The fact is, the public knows the current system of Division I athletics is corrupt and educationally bankrupt. Yet, they harbor little hope that higher education leaders have the courage and commitment to "do the right thing" and change it. If these leaders do not have the courage and commitment to reform athletics, how can we expect the public to trust them to do the right thing on any of the other important issues and challenges facing higher education and our society? Demonstrating visionary and progressive leadership in the area of athletics will profoundly impact the public's belief and trust in our nation's educational leaders and our system of higher education. With so many critical challenges facing American higher education and our culture, this is an opportunity that we can not afford to squander.

Although many in the athletics establishment will claim that the sky is falling, the risk of progressive, educationally motivated change is not nearly as great as we have been led to believe. The potential upside for higher education, however, is enormous. This is so because, on one level, eliminating the professional model will change very little. Undoubtedly, the relationship between the coach and the athlete, as well as the relationship between the school and the student, will change dramatically, which will require changes in the culture and operation of certain aspects of the enterprise. But these changes will occur mostly within the walls of the athletics department, far away from the bright lights and cheering of the fans. What the public sees and experiences will hardly change at all. Virtually every other constituent group with a stake in the enterprise—presidents, trustees, faculty, fans, alumni, and television networks and other media—will experience little, if any, impact.

The games will continue to be played. While they might be at a slightly lowered level of play, the difference will be hardly noticeable to the average fan. Fans and alumni will continue to return to campus to tailgate before games and gather under one roof to cheer for their favorite university teams. Newspapers will continue to write about, and radio talk-show hosts will continue to rant incessantly about, the games and the players who play them and the coaches who coach them. Television networks will continue to pay for the right to televise those games. Universities will continue to use sports events as a focal point of university gatherings and fundraising events. And athletics' potential as an instrument for institutional advancement will remain. All the public relations, university-advancement, community-building, fundraising, and entertainment benefits and functions will be unaffected by the elimination of the athletic scholarship as a way to de-professionalize the enterprise.

The fact is, the history and tradition associated with college athletics is so strong and has become so ingrained in the American culture that, regardless of whether the athletes receive athletic scholarships or whether the coach recruits off campus or whether there is spring football practice, the games and the pageantry will continue.

On another level, however, the change will be profound. Reforming the enterprise to conform more fully with the educational values of academe rather than the values of a professional sports franchise will enhance and strengthen that history and tradition. It will make it more genuine and honest. Moving Division I athletics away from the professional model toward one that is more compatible with the values and purposes of the educational institution will only strengthen its niche in the marketplace, its moral standing in our society, and its place in the fabric of American culture. In this increasingly jaded world, people want, indeed yearn, to believe in and be associated with something that is genuine, wholesome, and honest.

From an institutional-advancement standpoint, eliminating the department of professional athletics will present new and interesting opportunities. The challenge will be to effectively manage this reformed entity for maximum university gain. The progressive, structural changes advocated in these pages will provide the opportunity to rethink how higher education utilizes athletics' tremendous visibility and cultural influence to promote broader institutional goals and mission. A more genuine, educationally honest athletics program will actually increase athletics' value as a vehicle for promoting academic values and educational purposes. That being the case, higher education leaders must be prepared to recalibrate how this vehicle is utilized. From the way it is presented through television to the role and responsibilities of coaches as the most visible spokespeople for the university to the way the institution uses it in fundraising, eliminating the department of professional athletics will present many new, exciting, and challenging opportunities for higher education.

In short, de-professionalizing college athletics is not only the right thing to do from an educational standpoint, it is also the smart thing to do from a business perspective.

LOOKING FOR A SPARK

The need for and benefits of eliminating the professional athletics model from higher education are clear. As mentioned, the contextual environment within which college athletics operates has changed significantly. The critical mass of people, organizations, and institutions pushing for change is in place. These trends suggest that, despite the resistance from those who refuse to look beyond the status quo to a progressive future, the system can and will support the changes advocated in these pages. In fact, American higher education offers an excellent example of systemic change occurring against all odds. It was not very long ago that tenure was viewed as the one and only model for faculty employment. Tenure was considered a nonnegotiable faculty right and a foundation of the academic enterprise. Calls to change it were considered radical. Today, faculty tenure is viewed as one of many faculty employment models. Not all institutions offer tenure. Many colleges and universities conduct posttenure reviews. And institutions offering a two-track system of employment are not uncommon. In short, faculty tenure offers proof that American higher education is capable of initiating fundamental, systemic change when necessary.

Still, the question remains, What will be the spark to set into motion the process necessary to implement the types of reform advocated in these pages? There are two types of events that could provide such a spark; the first is reactive, while the second is proactive.

Many believe that there will come a point where one more widespread or particularly egregious athletic scandal will spark backlash of a nature that will either force such change or will result in the collapse of the entire system of big-time athletics. For example, a widespread gambling scandal or a particularly sordid academic fraud, fiscal, or drug-related scandal could be the straw that breaks the camel's back. It would be sad, however, if systemic reform were forced as a result of such a scandal. Rather than reacting to a negative event, it would be preferable for the higher education community to attack the issue aggressively and of its own free will. Why wait to respond to a crisis and have change rammed down one's throat when one can responsibly and proactively manage change?

With a foundation that will support systemic change in place, a growing critical mass of individuals, organizations, and institutions pushing for change, and a contextual environment that will contribute to and support such change, it will not take much to start and follow through on the process. All it would take would be a handful of visionary, progressive college presidents to start the ball rolling. If, for example, a group of ten presidents from schools that the public believes have the most to lose from such change were to boldly step forward to demand reform, the process would snowball. Imagine what would happen if the presidents from schools such as the University of Michigan; University of Florida; University of Kansas; University of California, Los Angeles; Stanford University; Ohio State University; University of North Carolina; University of Texas; University of Nebraska; and University of Miami came together in a steadfast manner and demanded that American higher education eliminate the professional model of athletics from the academy? Because these schools are so "successful" under the current system and are viewed as having the most to lose, the rest of the higher education community would follow their lead. Such a scenario is not as far-fetched as it may seem. According to a 2005 *Chronicle of Higher Education* survey, 59 percent of college presidents say that "big-time college athletics is more of a liability than an asset."

More likely, however, is that a group of presidents will work through the NCAA committee structure to drive such change. The NCAA Presidential Task Force on the Future of Division I Intercollegiate Athletics, formed in January 2005, offers the potential for such leadership. Its charge is to explore the alignment of intercollegiate athletics with the mission, values, and goals of higher education in such areas as fiscal responsibility, commercialism, organizational structure, and transparency of athletics operations.

Eliminating the athletic scholarship would be the most effective way to address all of these concerns. Changing to a need-based aid system should significantly reduce budgets. Further, without scholarships and the professional-franchise mentality it spawns, there would be no need for off-campus recruiting, ever-expanding coaching staffs and administrative positions, and over-the-top, palatial facilities. With the growth of expenditures far exceeding new revenues, the fiscal foundation of the current professional model is simply unsustainable. Elimination of the athletic scholarship and the dismantling of the professional model would restore a level of sanity to athletics' fiscal operations.

Further, these changes, coupled with the changes to institutional structure suggested in chapter 6, would address the task force's charge regarding organizational structure on two levels. Not only would these progressive reforms address the issue of university structure relating to athletics, they would also have a profound cultural effect on the institution. It is no secret that Division I athletics departments, due to their professionalized values, culture, and operations, exist as separate and distinct entities, apart from the academic culture and institution. By eliminating the foundation of the professional model, an institution's ability to integrate athletes into the student body, coaches into the faculty community, and the athletics department into the fabric of the university could become a reality. When this reintegration occurs, transparency in athletics operations will follow.

Finally, as mentioned, it is not commercialism that is at the root of college athletics' ills but rather the model higher education has chosen to reap athletics' commercial potential. The elimination of the professional model would provide an excellent opportunity for American higher education to revisit its use of athletics' commercial potential and to restructure it in a way that is more compatible with institutional values and mission and, in the process, strengthen it as a powerful educational, fundraising, and public relations resource.

In other words, the "tipping point" for such change may not be as far away as one might imagine. It will only take the visionary and courageous leadership of a handful of presidents and trustees to forever change the face of American education. It is undoubtedly in higher education's best interest to act in a proactive way, as opposed to being forced to respond to the widespread public outcry from faculty, media, politicians, and fans that will result when "one too many scandals" erupts. And make no mistake about it: that scandal, or court case, or congressional action will occur. We simply can not continue down our current path of increasing professionalism of college athletics. The values and operating principles of the professional sports model are simply too incongruous with the values and operating principles of higher education. At some point, the system will no longer be able to support the hypocrisy that looms over the entire enterprise. And, like a deck of cards, it will collapse.

LEADERSHIP AND THE WILL TO ACT

American higher education is at a crossroads regarding the role that athletics plays in our nation's educational system. Given higher education's influence in our society, how it responds to this challenge will be felt at the high school, junior high, and community levels. Central to that decision-making process is the need to understand, confirm, and appreciate the difference between what we *do* in college athletics, which is conduct games, and what we are *about*, which is education. Games, statistics, and scores are relatively meaningless. Newspaper clippings fade, trophies tarnish, and, by the time this year's championship game is played, most people will have forgotten who participated in last year's. What has lasting significance, however, is the way in which athletics can positively impact educational institutions and those who play and watch. If this distinction is not clearly understood and fully embraced by the higher education community—not simply through rhetoric but by action—college athletics will continue to be trivialized as simply entertainment, with no deeper or more compelling rationale for its existence other than that it provides a place to watch a game on Saturday afternoon.

In the previous pages we have reviewed the fundamental justifications for American education's experiment with elite athletics. We have also identified the many ways in which that experiment has failed and the resultant negative impact of that failure on our colleges, high schools, communities, and our cultural values and priorities.

But to simply criticize the current system without offering an alternative is irresponsible. Thus, the European club model of sports was identified as a model that will more effectively utilize athletics as a tool for educational and public health purposes. While it is helpful to identify and visualize an alternative model, one also needs a road map or plan for achieving that model. Given higher education's leadership responsibility in our culture, the road begins in our colleges and universities. And the fundamental change that must occur is the elimination of the professional model of athletics, with the athletic scholarship as its foundation, from higher education.

That said, the question remains, Can this be achieved? Many believe change of the magnitude suggested in this book is impossible. I disagree. As outlined, the time for systemic change has never been better. The context against which the reform efforts are being played out is significantly different than at any other time in the history of American higher education. There is a momentum for change that has been building since 1982 when a group of presidents demanded that athletes perform in the classroom as well as on the field. Along the way, other individuals, groups, commissions, and organizations have come to appreciate the importance of reforming athletics and have become increasingly engaged with the issue. As a result, the critical mass of ideas, people, organizations, processes, commissions, and circumstances that is necessary to drive cultural change has been coalescing. Athletics reform efforts can no longer be thought of as a passing higher education fancy. After twenty-four years of continued presidential engagement, athletics reform has become a full-fledged movement.

Past reform efforts have, for the most part, achieved limited success because those efforts have largely been in response to a specific crisis or a series of scandals. Generally, a few measures designed to curb the specific abuse or abuses are adopted and the college athletics enterprise moves on to business as usual. Further, such efforts have focused on the symptoms, such as low graduation rates, rather than the root cause of the problems, the system itself. Not surprisingly, past reform efforts have been short term, difficult to sustain, and have resulted in little systemic change.

A movement, however, is proactive in nature; a drive to change a system. Movements are predicated on the desire of a critical mass of people and institutions coalescing to bear the pressure necessary to change a fundamentally flawed system. Movements are founded on the idea that the nature of the problem is the system itself.

Despite the critical assessment of the current state of athletics in America and past attempts to reform it, this is a hopeful book. It is hopeful because there is a place for elite athletics in America. It is hopeful because college athletics is not a flawed enterprise. Rather, it is the model higher education has chosen to reap the academic and institutional-advancement potential of athletics that is flawed. Once we openly acknowledge what we know to be true, it becomes clear that athletics reform is about a choice. Do we continue to sponsor a department of professional athletics, despite the fact that it continues to undermine academic values and institutional mission in very damaging ways, or do we eliminate it from the academy?

Three additional points are clear. First, there is no longer any lack of information or understanding of the problems associated with the professional brand of college athletics. There is simply too much data and evidence to continue to explain away these problems as short term or limited in scope. No reasonable person can look at the facts and conclude that the current system of professional athletics on campus is not broken. Second, presidents, with the support of their boards and working through their faculties, must provide the leadership to drive this change. And finally, presidents not only have the clear authority but now also the means by which to implement this change, as there is no longer any doubt that presidents control the NCAA legislative and governance process. Presidents can reform athletics in any way they please because they have the ability, the process, the authority, and a growing critical mass of people and organizations to help them do so. The system can handle the change.

The fact is, higher education built the system and higher education can change it. Or, as Derek Bok writes in *Universities in the Marketplace* (2003), "Priorities on a campus are not immutable. If they seem so, it is often because too little effort has been made to change them" (p. 184).

In the final analysis, systemic athletics reform is no longer a theoretical exercise. It has become a matter of having the will and the courage to dismantle an operation that has come to represent values and practices that are diametrically opposed to progressive academic values and the educational mission of the institution and to restructure it in a way that fits more comfortably into the fabric of the institution.

In *Casablanca*'s final scene, as they walk off into the foggy evening, Rick utters the memorable refrain, "Louie, I think this is the beginning of a beautiful relationship." When the professional model of athletics was formally incorporated into American higher education, it was fully expected that the partnership would be as beautiful and mutually beneficial as Louie and Rick's. Unfortunately, more than a century later, a more fitting commentary is "It's time to end this relationship and build a more sensible one."

The table of reform is set. The pieces are all in place. The system can support the change. The question is whether we have the courage to change it.

CHRONOLOGY OF COLLEGE ATHLETICS REFORM INITIATIVES

1895

The president of Purdue University calls together the presidents from the University of Illinois, the University of Michigan, the University of Minnesota, Northwestern University, and the University of Wisconsin to establish the Intercollegiate Conference of Faculty Representatives.

1905

President Theodore Roosevelt summons college athletics leaders to two White House conferences to encourage reforms in the sport of football due to several deaths and serious injuries in the sport.

Henry M. MacCracken, chancellor of New York University, convenes a meeting of thirteen institutions to initiate changes in football, resulting in the eventual formation of the Intercollegiate Athletic Association of the United States (IAAUS) in 1906, the forerunner of the NCAA. The association has sixty-two founding members. This body is conceived as an educational body with no legislative authority.

1910

The Intercollegiate Athletic Association of the United States adopts its present name, the National Collegiate Athletic Association (NCAA).

1929

The Carnegie Foundation releases a report claiming many instances of recruitment and subsidization of athletes and several cases where athletic departments are not under faculty control and are unduly influenced by alumni and coaches.

1934

The NCAA adopts a code on the recruiting and subsidization of athletes. Implementation of this code, however, rests with individual conferences. The NCAA's role continues to be advisory in nature.

1946

NCAA adopts the "Sanity Code," which outlines principles for recruitment, amateurism, sound academic standards, and the awarding of financial aid. Further, the membership passes a resolution giving the NCAA the authority to establish a rules enforcement mechanism as a means of implementing the Sanity Code.

1951

College presidents determine that the NCAA requires a full-time executive director and a permanent headquarters.

1952

The NCAA Convention establishes an NCAA Membership Committee to consider complaints of failure to comply with the rules or its constitution and adopts regulatory legislation governing the administration of financial aid to athletes.

The American Council on Education releases a report from a special committee of presidents. The report calls for more stringent eligibility standards, basing financial aid awards to athletes on academic achievement and economic need and prohibiting freshman eligibility.

1954

Presidents, through their institutional vote at the NCAA Convention, give more authority and power to the NCAA by approving the establishment of a Committee on Infractions to consolidate all investigations and provide a more comprehensive approach to regulation and enforcement. The long-standing principle of faculty control is emphasized as being the first step in any regulatory process.

1961

Presidents obligate member institutions to apply and enforce NCAA legislation and direct that the enforcement program apply to any member institution that fails to fulfill this obligation.

1965

NCAA adopts the "1.600 rule," which establishes a minimum GPA for eligibility for NCAA championships and financial aid.

1973

NCAA abolishes the 1.600 rule in favor of a rule requiring that athletes graduate from high school with a 2.00 GPA to be eligible for NCAA championships and financial aid.

1981

In response to scandals involving the doctoring of academic records, the NCAA votes to require athletes to complete a specific number of credit hours each term to remain eligible for varsity sports.

The traditionally all-male NCAA establishes new women's championships and develops plans to create policies to govern both men's and women's sports.

1982

A group of presidents, working through the American Council on Education, proposes more stringent eligibility standards for incoming freshmen athletes.

1983

NCAA Division I votes to toughen academic standards for freshmen athletes, requiring them to meet minimum standardized-test score requirements and earn at least a 2.0 grade point average in a high school curriculum. The rule, commonly known as Proposition 48, passes despite bitter opposition from black college presidents who claim the inclusion of test score requirements would make the standards discriminatory.

1984

The NCAA Presidents Commission of forty-four members is established. The committee is empowered to:

1. Review any activity of the association
2. Place any matter of concern on the agenda of any meeting of the NCAA Council or of any NCAA convention

3. Study intercollegiate athletics issues and urge certain courses of action
4. Propose legislation directly to any NCAA convention
5. Establish the final sequence of legislative proposals in any convention agenda
6. Call for a special meeting of the association
7. Designate, prior to the printing of the notice of any convention, specific proposals for which a roll-call vote would be mandatory

1985

The Presidents Commission initiates eight legislative proposals and calls for an NCAA Special Convention, which passes all eight proposals. Among these proposals are the following:

1. Athletics budgets controlled by the institution and subject to its normal budgeting procedures
2. Annual audits of all expenditures for the athletics program by an outside, independent auditor
3. A self-study of each institution's athletics program at least once every five years
4. Requirement of Division I members to report graduation rates of athletes
5. A "repeat offender" provision, allowing the Committee on Infractions to impose the "death penalty" on a program if that or another program within the department has committed major violations within the previous five years
6. More stringent enforcement procedures and penalties
7. Requirement that restrictions imposed on a coach by the Committee on Infractions be applied to that coach even if he or she moves to another member institution

The president of Tulane University announces that the university will abolish its men's basketball program, which is beset by recruiting violations and allegations of gambling. The program will be reinstated in 1989.

1986

Proposition 48 takes effect.

Presidents Commission authorizes the creation of the NCAA Legislative Services Department to improve rules education and interpretation services.

1987

The Infractions Committee, for the first time, imposes its "death penalty" for repeat violators, barring Southern Methodist University from playing football for a year and restricting its schedule for another year. The penalties are the harshest ever issued for rules violations in college football.

Dick Schultz is hired as NCAA Executive Director, replacing Walter Byers, who had held the position since 1951.

1988

Results of Presidents Commission-sponsored research on athlete welfare are released. The study finds that athletes are spending over thirty hours per week on athletic activities, entering college with significantly lower test scores and high school grades, not performing nearly as well academically as nonathletes, and feeling "isolated" from the campus community.

1989

"Simplified" NCAA manual is introduced.

NCAA Student-Athlete Advisory Committee is established.

Presidents establish a $3.5 million fund for Division I conferences to improve compliance efforts, basketball officiating, drug education programs, and opportunities for ethnic minorities and women.

NCAA creates Compliance Department to assist schools in developing systems of checks and balances to ensure more effective oversight of athletic department operations.

Presidents Commission authorizes the exploration of the development of a certification program for athletic departments. A two-year pilot program is established to determine the feasibility, expense, and potential effectiveness of such a program.

The Knight Commission on Intercollegiate Athletics is established.

1990

NCAA Executive Director Dick Schultz calls for the development of a "new model" of intercollegiate athletics in his "State of the Association Address."

College Sports Inc.: The Athletic Department versus the University, by Murray Sperber, is released. The book focuses on the emerging corporate form of intercollegiate athletics and its enormous financial and ethical cost to American higher education.

1991

Athletes' graduation rates are publicly reported.

NCAA Student-Athlete Welfare Convention results in several significant changes, including:

1. A rule limiting athletes to twenty hours of athletically related activities per week
2. A rule eliminating athletic dormitories
3. A rule shortening playing seasons

Presidents Commission revises formula for distributing revenue from the men's basketball tournament to include factors other than a team's performance in the tournament.

L. Jay Oliva, chancellor of the State University of New York, prepares a paper for the Knight Commission entitled "10 Commandments of Presidential Behavior on Athletics."

The Knight Commission on Intercollegiate Athletics releases its initial report, entitled *Keeping Faith with the Student-Athlete: A New Model for Intercollegiate Athletics*. The report outlines a "one plus three" model for athletic reform with the one—presidential control—directed toward the three—academic integrity, fiscal integrity, and independent certification.

The presidents of Big 10 Conference institutions wield their influence over the conference's television contract with ESPN. Big 10 schools will no longer play basketball games starting at 9:30 PM on Monday nights, but instead move to a 7:30 PM time slot on Tuesdays.

The Presidents Commission supports legislation mandating that coaches receive annual prior written approval from their chief executive officer for all contracts for athletically related income and benefits from sources outside the institution.

The United States House Subcommittee on Commerce, Consumer Protection and Competitiveness holds ten hearings about college sports, covering issues relating to financing and governance of big-time college sports, including the power of presidents in the NCAA and the fairness of the NCAA's investigative process.

1992

The Presidents Commission supports and NCAA adopts legislation that raises initial eligibility standards under which athletes will have to complete thirteen core courses (up from eleven) with a GPA of 2.50 (up from 2.00). The provision is to be effective in 1995.

NCAA Division I adopts new requirements stipulating minimum percentages of credits earned toward a specific degree, as well as a minimum GPA toward that degree, for athletes' third and fourth years of
eligibility, effective 1996. Further, the permissible number of credits
earned during the summer to maintain eligibility is capped.

The Knight Commission on Intercollegiate Athletics releases its second
report, entitled *A Solid Start: A Report on Reform of Intercollegiate
Athletics.*

The NCAA amends its constitution to require presidential approval of
conference-sponsored legislation.

1993

Nearly every proposal favored by the Presidents Commission wins
approval from delegates at the NCAA Convention, and almost every
proposal the presidents opposed is defeated. Presidents Commission
measures that are passed include the adoption of the certification program as well as the creation of a Joint Policy Board that gives presidents more say over the NCAA's budget and other business.

The Knight Commission releases what, at the time, is to be its final
report, entitled *A New Beginning for a New Century: Intercollegiate
Athletics in the United States.* The report acknowledges that the struggle for reform is far from over and identifies a few areas as continued
trouble spots, including recruiting abuses, the influence of the entertainment culture on athletics, the compulsion of boosters to meddle in
athletics department decision making, and failure to respect the dig-
nity of athletes.

1995

The NCAA Certification Program takes effect, with sixty Division I
institutions starting the year-long process.

NCAA adopts the "Principles of Student-Athlete Welfare."

Presidents Commission endorses legislation that would overhaul the
association's governance system. The plan restructures the NCAA
by giving more autonomy to each division and final decision-making
authority to presidents.

Initial eligibility requiring thirteen core course (up from eleven) with a
GPA of 2.50 (up from 2.0) becomes effective.

Unsportsmanlike Conduct: Exploiting College Athletes, a scathing critique of the increasing commercialization of college athletics, written by former NCAA executive director Walter Byers, is released.

1996

NCAA adopts a governance restructuring plan that puts presidents clearly in charge of NCAA decision making and gives divisions more control over their own affairs. The association's top body, the Executive Committee, is comprised entirely of CEOs and the NCAA's three divisions are led by presidential groups. Division I moves away from the one-institution-one-vote concept in favor of a representative system, in which decisions are made by committees and councils. Divisions II and III retain the one-institution-one-vote governance format.

NCAA adopts a higher minimum percentage of degree requirements for all junior college transfers in Division I football and men's basketball. These athletes will have to complete 35 percent—versus 25 percent—of their degree requirements to be immediately eligible in their third year of enrollment.

Legislation requiring minimum percentages of credits earned toward a specific degree, as well as a minimum GPA toward that degree, for athletes' third and fourth years of eligibility becomes effective.

The Knight Commission dissolves but notes that it would be watching "with an interested eye" to see how college presidents handle the new overall powers voted to them.

1997

Governance restructuring plan becomes effective.

Darwin's Athletes: How Sport Has Damaged Black America and Preserved the Myth of Race is released. Written by John Hoberman, the book articulates how our nation's fixation on black athletic achievement has come to play a disastrous role in African-American life and a troubling role in our country's race relations.

1998

By design, presidents do not pursue any major reform legislation in 1998 as they want to let the NCAA adjust to the newly restructured legislation and governance system.

College Athletes for Hire: The Evolution and Legacy of the NCAA's Amateur Myth, coauthored by Allen Sack and Ellen Staurowsky is released.

1999

Organized forces for reform external to the traditional NCAA structure begin to emerge, most notably, the Drake Group, a group of faculty members from across the country with the goal of restoring academic integrity to intercollegiate athletics. Their agenda includes:

1. Remove academic counseling for athletes from the control of athletic departments.
2. Publicly disclose information about majors, advisors, and courses taken by all athletes without revealing individual grades.
3. Eliminate athletic scholarships and expand need-based aid for all students. This position has been since modified to making the athletic scholarship a five-year, rather than the current one-year, agreement.
4. Reduce the number of athletic contests.
5. Stop using the term "student-athlete" and instead refer to those who participate in athletics as either students or athletes.

Unpaid Professionals: Commercialism and Conflict in Big-Time College Sports, by Andrew Zimbalist, is released.

2000

The NCAA Division I Board of Directors calls for strong action to deal with problems in college basketball and announces that the association will adopt more stringent steps than many had previously thought. This includes a measure that penalizes universities that graduate less than 50 percent of their basketball players with the loss of a scholarship.

The Knight Commission on Intercollegiate Athletics reconvenes to report on the changes that have occurred in the decade since its recommendations were made, evaluating how well they worked and whether new recommendations are warranted.

Indiana University president Myles Brand fires legendary basketball coach Bobby Knight.

Led by a group of former athletes, the Collegiate Athletes Coalition is formed to improve the lives and conditions of college athletes, with an emphasis on financial issues, including a call to raise the amount of an athletic scholarship to cover the full cost of attendance and to ensure that health coverage for athletes extended out of season.

Beer and Circus: How Big-Time College Sports Is Crippling Undergraduate Education, by Murray Sperber, and *Intercollegiate Athletics and the American University: A University President's Perspective*, by former president of the University of Michigan James Duderstadt, are released.

2001

The Knight Commission releases a report entitled *A Call to Action: Reconnecting College Sports and Higher Education*. The commission indicates that athletic reform is no longer simply about institutional integrity and higher education; rather, its influence has come to negatively influence the entire American culture of sport. The report calls for "a concerted grassroots effort by the broader academic community—in concert with trustees, administrators and faculty—to restore the balance of athletics and academics on campus" (Knight Foundation Commission on Intercollegiate Athletics, 2001a, p. 23).

The Game of Life: College Sports and Educational Values, by James Shulman and William Bowen, is released.

2002

The Coalition on Intercollegiate Athletics, a group of faculty leaders from over fifty Division I-A institutions, forms as an e-mail network. In 2003, COIA evolves into a coalition of faculty senates welcoming members from all Division I-A schools. Its purpose is to position itself as a faculty voice in the national debate over college athletics.

In response to the Knight Commission's call for governing boards "to do more to help resolve the persistent problems" addressed in its 2001 report, the Association of Governing Boards' (AGB) board of directors authorizes the development of a statement designed to provide governing boards with principles to help guide them in their governance responsibilities concerning athletics.

The American Association of University Professors publishes a "best practices" document for its membership entitled *The Faculty Role in the Reform of Intercollegiate Athletics: Principles and Recommended Practices*.

2003

Indiana University president Myles Brand is hired as NCAA president. He is the first former university president to head the organization.

The National Institute for Sports Reform is established. NISR is a coalition of educators, members of the media, and various sports reformers devoted to studying, advocating, and implementing sports reform measures at the youth, amateur, scholastic, and collegiate levels.

Knight Commission on Intercollegiate Athletics convenes for a third time, citing concerns regarding increasing commercialization of college athletics, and indicates that it will serve its "watchdog" function and issue periodic reports on the state of college athletics.

The American Association of University Professors continues its efforts to define and develop faculty responsibilities and practices relating to athletics by developing series of guidelines for "The Appointment and Function of Faculty Athletics Representatives," "Standards for the Appointment and Function of Campus Athletics Committees," and "Guidelines for Institutional Governance and Intercollegiate Athletics."

Claiming the Game: College Sports and Educational Values, by William Bowen and Sarah Levin, is released. It is a follow-up to *The Game of Life* and raises serious questions regarding the role that athletics plays on campuses.

2004

The Association of Governing Boards releases a "best practices" document designed to encourage trustees to become more responsibly engaged in the oversight and governance of athletic programs on their campuses.

The United States Senate Judiciary Committee convenes hearings on the football Bowl Championship Series and the commercialization of college athletics.

2005

NCAA adopts a major academic reform package designed to penalize a team with the loss of scholarships and eligibility for postseason play if its athletes continue to perform at substandard academic levels.

REFERENCES

Araton, Harvey. 2005. "College or Pros? Answer Seems Driven by Race." *New York Times*, 26 July, C-19.

Arone, Michael. 2002. "State Spending on Colleges Increases at Lowest Rate in a Decade." *Chronicle of Higher Education*, 13 December, A-28.

Bissinger, H. G. 1990. *Friday Night Lights: A Town, a Team, and a Dream*. New York: Addison Wesley.

Bok, Derek. 2003. *Universities in the Marketplace: The Commercialization of Higher Education*. Princeton, NJ: Princeton University Press.

Bowen, William G., and Sarah A. Levin. 2003. *Reclaiming the Game: College Sports and Educational Values*. Princeton, NJ: Princeton University Press.

Brand, Myles. 2004. "State of the Association Address." Delivered at the NCAA Convention, Nashville, Tenn. 11 January.

———. 2005a. "Faculty Input Integral to Instilling Integrity within Academic Reform." *NCAA News*, 14 February, 4+.

———. 2005b. "*State of the Association Address.*" *NCAA News*, 17 January, A-4.

Coleman, James S. 1961. *The Adolescent Society: The Social Life of the Teenager and Its Impact on Education*. New York: Free Press.

College Board. 2002. *Trends in College Pricing*. New York: College Board.

Everson, Garry. 2002. E-mail to author, 8 October.

Falla, Jack. 1981. *NCAA: The Voice of College Sports: A Diamond Anniversary History, 1906–1981*. Mission, KS: National Collegiate Athletic Association. Mission, KS.

Flannery, Tim. 2002. Telephone conversation with the author, 21 November.

Friedman, Thomas L. 2005. "Where Have You Gone Joe DiMaggio?" *New York Times*, 13 May, A-23.

Fulks, Daniel L. 2001. *Revenues and Expenses of Division I and II Intercollegiate Athletics Programs: Financial Trends and Relationships—2001*. Indianapolis, IN: National Collegiate Athletic Association.

Gerdy, John. 1997. *The Successful College Athletic Program: The New Standard*. American Council on Education Series on Higher Education. Phoenix, AZ: Oryx Press.

———. 2000. *Sports in School: The Future of an Institution*. New York: Teachers College Press-Columbia University.

Gerdy, John R. 2002. *Sports: The All-American Addiction*. Jackson: University Press of Mississippi.

Gerdy, John R., Ellen Staurowsky, and Bruce Svare. 2004. *2004 NCAA Division I Men's and Women's Basketball Coaches' Academic Degree Survey*. Selkirk, NY: National Institute for Sports Reform.

Gladwell, Malcolm. 2000. *The Tipping Point: How Little Things Can Make a Big Difference*. Boston: Back Bay Books.

Gross, Mike. 1999. *Lancaster Intelligencer-Journal*, 14 February, C-6.

Hiestand, Michael. 2003. "Politicians Join BCS Debate and We All Sleep a Bit Better." *USA Today*, 30 October, 2-C.

Institute for International Sport. 1999–2000. *Men's College Basketball Sportsmanship Research*. Kingston, R.I.: University of Rhode Island.

Knight Foundation Commission on Intercollegiate Athletics. 2001a. *A Call to Action: Reconnecting College Sports and Higher Education*. Miami, FL: John S. and James L. Knight Foundation.

———. 2001b. Hearings, Washington, D.C. Transcript. Miami, FL: John S. and James L. Knight Foundation. 23 January.

———. 2003. Hearings, Washington, D.C. Transcript. Miami, FL.: John S. and James L. Knight Foundation. 14 November.

———. 1991. *Keeping Faith with the Student-Athlete: A New Model for Intercollegiate Athletics*. Charlotte, NC: John S. and James L. Knight Foundation. March.

Kralovec, Etta. 2003. *Schools That Do Too Much: Wasting Time and Money in Schools and What We All Can Do about It*. Boston: Beacon Press.

Lombardi Program on Measuring University Performance. 2003. *The Top American Research Universities*. Gainesville: University of Florida.

McCabe, Robert. 2000. "The Rise of American Sport and the Decline of American Culture." In *Sports in School: The Future of an Institution*, edited by John R. Gerdy. New York: Teachers College Press-Columbia University.

McGovern, Mike. 2005. E-mail to author, 23 May.

Miracle, Andrew W., and C. Roger Rees. 1994. *Lessons of the Locker Room: The Myth of School Sports*. Amherst, N.Y.: Prometheus Books.

National Collegiate Athletic Association (NCAA). 1991. *The Public and the Media's Understanding and Assessment of the NCAA*. Poll conducted by Louis Harris and Associates, New York: NCAA.

———. 2000a. "Chronological History of Presidential Involvement in Intercollegiate Athletics." 21 December. Indianapolis, IN: NCAA.

———. 2000b. *NCAA Response to Knight Commission Recommendations*. 6 July. Indianapolis, IN: NCAA.

———. 2002. *The Will to Act*. Indianapolis, IN: NCAA.

"New Approach to Childhood Obesity Is Urged." 2004. *New York Times*, 1 October, A-20.

Patterson, Cynthia. 2000. "Athletics and the Higher Education Marketplace." In *Sports in School: The Future of an Institution*, edited by John R. Gerdy. New York: Teachers College Press–Columbia University.

Pennington, Bill. 2004. "NCAA Set to Put Teeth in Academic Guidelines." *New York Times*, 29 April, C-17.

———. 2005. "Doctors See a Big Rise in Injuries for Young Athletes." *New York Times*, 22 February, Sports section, 1.

Porto, Brian L. 2003. *A New Season: Using Title IX to Reform College Sports*. Westport, CT: Praeger.

Putnam, Douglas T. 1999. *Controversies of the Sports World*. Westport, CT: Greenwood Press.

Reed, Ken. 2004. "Back Talk; Elitism in Youth Sports Yields Physical Fatness." *New York Times*, 1 February, Sports section, 1.

Rhoden, William. 2004. "Once Again, Reform Misses the Real Problem." *New York Times*, 29 April, C-17+.

———. 2005. "A Knack for Making Good Moves." *New York Times*, 21 March, D-1.

Roberts, Gary. 1994. "Consider Everything Else before Restructuring." *NCAA News*, 19 September, 4–5.

Rothstein, Richard. 2000. "Do New Standards in the Three R's Crowd Out P.E.?" *New York Times*, 29 November, A-29.

Sack, Allen L., and Ellen J. Staurowsky. 1998. *College Athletes for Hire: The Evolution and Legacy of the NCAA's Amateur Myth.* Westport, CT: Praeger.

Schemo, Diana Jean. 2002. "Public College Tuition Rises 10 Percent amid Financial Cuts." *New York Times*, 22 October, A-18.

Shulman, James L., and William G. Bowen. 2001. *The Game of Life: College Sports and Educational Values.* Princeton, NJ: Princeton University Press.

Suggs, Welch. 2001. "Study Casts Doubt on Idea the Winning Teams Yield More Applicants." *Chronicle of Higher Education*, 30 March, A-51.

———. 2003. "Knight Commission Reconvenes to Discuss Problems in College Sports." *Chronicle of Higher Education*, 25 November, p. 1 [Online]. Available: http://chronicle.com/daily/2003/11/2003112501n.htm [25 November 2003].

———. 2004. "The Chronicle Survey of Public Opinion on Higher Education." *Chronicle of Higher Education*, 7 May, A-12.

Summers, Ellen. 2004. E-mail to author, 22 March.

Watterson, John Sayle. 2000. *College Football: History, Spectacle, Controversy.* Baltimore, MD: Johns Hopkins Press.

"What Presidents Think." 2005. *Chronicle of Higher Education*, 4 November, A-27.

Zimbalist, Andrew, and Roger G. Noll. 1997. *Sports, Jobs, and Taxes: The Economic Impact of Sports Teams and Stadiums.* Washington, D.C.: Brookings Institution Press.

INDEX